EVERYONE DIES,
BUT NOT
EVERYONE LIVES

EVERYONE DIES, BUT NOT EVERYONE LIVES

developing a personal rule for life

M. S. BICKFORD

LEAFWOOD
PUBLISHERS

an imprint of Abilene Christian University Press

EVERYONE DIES, BUT NOT EVERYONE LIVES
Developing a Personal Rule for Life

LEAFWOOD
P U B L I S H E R S
an imprint of Abilene Christian University Press

Copyright © 2015 by M. S. Bickford

ISBN 978-0-89112-462-7

Printed in the United States of America

Published in association with the Seymour Agency, 475 Miner Street Road, Canton, NY 13617.

Cover design by Elizabeth Fulton | Cover photo by Kayce McClure
Interior text design by Sandy Armstrong, Strong Design

For information contact:
Abilene Christian University Press
ACU Box 29138
Abilene, Texas 79699

1-877-816-4455
www.leafwoodpublishers.com

15 16 17 18 19 20 / 7 6 5 4 3 2 1

To Lenore and Stuart Kniff,
who started me on this journey
and to Ruth and Rich Grobe,
who made sure I was able to finish it.

Contents

Preface

This book is the result of a life-long effort to grow as a Christian. I have never found myself content to just stay put. I have always sought to continually grow and deepen my understanding of the hold Jesus Christ has on my life and how he shapes the lives of his followers as we make our way through this world.

We are each called to a pilgrimage that takes us to places of growth, pain, discovery, suffering, triumph, failure, and, most importantly, to deeper faith. The pace of our progress also varies greatly over time. There are times when we feel like we are reaching a new spiritual mountaintop every day, and there are times when we spend years in the dark valley without being able to see the way out. Each of these experiences shapes us and influences the direction of our lives to some degree.

I have always seen the objective of this pilgrimage as straightforward: to become more and more Christlike and to serve his church according to the call he has given to me. The destination, in some ways, is the easy part. The hard part for me is the journey to get there. It is a journey during which I have consistently crossed paths with unexpected people and events. It is where I have dealt with the ghosts of my family and with the mistakes and failings of my own life. It is also where I have been influenced by others whom God has placed in my path and where I have learned the most. This journey has gone from the high of seeing the pride in my parents' eyes when I completed a PhD at a prestigious Jesuit university in only three years to the low of working third shift stocking shelves at a department store six months later because I could not find a teaching job.

My own pilgrimage has been an amazing one, but I have often failed to learn important lessons and have been forced to retrace steps that could have been avoided if only I had understood what happened the first time around. There has been necessary suffering, but there has also been needless suffering for people who should not have been hurt along the way. Had there been more guidance and clarity, I could have avoided some of the self-inflicted pain and more quickly learned the lessons that instead needed to be learned over and over again.

This book is not about the destination, but about helping you in your own pilgrimage. Some people undertake the journey with excitement and commitment, while others would prefer to sit at a café with like-minded friends and tell the same stories and jokes over and over. To be on a pilgrimage is to be on the path of growth and to understand the lessons God is teaching. To stay put is to remain unchanged by our encounters with life and to die not having accomplished what God has put us on earth to do. Undertaking a pilgrimage means knowing where it will lead, but having no clue what we will encounter while on it—and that is the true adventure of life!

The goal of this book is to help you be more intentional and systematic about your spiritual development. It does not take a cookbook approach, where the addition of certain ingredients in a certain order will produce a specific and predictable result. It is also not a direct map of the journey, but rather a collection of tools that can be used to help you on your pilgrimage.

If you take the time to wrestle with the questions I pose herein, and pray deeply about how to develop your own Rule for Life, this book can be of immense assistance. However, please know that a Rule for Life is not the answer; faithfulness to the pilgrimage of Christian faith is. The Rule is just a tool to help, and it will need to be regularly revisited and revised to incorporate the lessons you learn.

When I look back at my own pilgrimage, there are so many people that have influenced and shaped me over the years. Friends who have shared the journey, teachers who have patiently worked with me, mentors who have offered invaluable guidance, colleagues who have walked beside me in the valleys, parishioners who have invited me to help them with their pilgrimages, and students who have trusted my help. To list them all would take far more space than is permitted, but I hope you know how much gratitude and love I have for you! It is amazing just how helpful a conversation or word of encouragement can be at the right moment. To share this pilgrimage of faith and life with others is an incredible blessing!

For the publication of this book, I want to thank Mary Sue Seymour, my literary agent, and Mary Hardegree, my editor at Leafwood Publishers, for their guidance, help, and support.

Taking on a first-time author is a risky decision, and I will be eternally grateful to both of you for the faith you have in me! I also want to thank my family for their support. You have taught me well and kept me grounded. Additionally, my children have taught me more about theology and humanity than any professor ever could!

When my time on earth is done, I do not wish to stand before God having lived a comfortable life or having followed a safe religion. I hope to arrive in heaven with a worn out body, a heart overflowing with the memories of the lives I've touched, and a deep gratitude for all who have affected and shaped me! There will certainly be a lot for us to share and talk about!

M. S. Bickford
On the 19th anniversary of my ordination
July 23, 2014

1

What Is Life?

"Life is either a daring adventure or nothing."

—Helen Keller, *The Open Door*

Jeff had a small "X" tattooed on three spots on his scalp. What was left of his hair failed to cover the marks, but the markers for the radiation treatments were the least of his problems. At sixty-nine years old, he was going to die and he knew it.

Jeff grew up in a working class section of Newark and was able to get a job with a utility company right out of high school. His work was tedious, and he often worked outside in inclement weather. The good news was that he earned enough money to provide a modest living for his family. Over the years, he did his work, followed the union in times of labor disputes, and worked overtime when the opportunities arose. He was able to send his children to parochial school and then, with the help of student

13

loans, to college. Ambition was not part of his formula for life. He never wrestled with questions of meaning. He knew that God was important, but he had never sought God. He knew that education was important, but he never sought to grow. Other than making sure that the bills were paid and that the children stayed out of trouble, his only goal was to reach retirement so that he could golf and sail on his small boat.

Six months before retirement, he started feeling a little off. Jeff assumed that he was just tired and that the break from getting up at 4:45 every morning would do the trick. His retirement finally came, and the party his friends threw for him was wonderful. A few weeks later, as he struggled with headaches and a strange problem with his sense of balance, he started to think that he should go to the doctor. But you know how that goes, even with persistent nagging from his spouse. More time passed before he finally made the appointment.

The next eighteen months flew by. Instead of golfing and sailing, most of that time was spent fighting brain cancer. He had surgery to remove a tumor and underwent an aggressive round of chemotherapy and radiation. The struggle took its toll, but something amazing happened. As I pushed Jeff through his neighborhood one day in his wheelchair for some fresh air, he began to share his thoughts with me. As he contemplated his approaching death, he began to think about life and its purpose. He wondered out loud about why he had never thought of these matters before. It wasn't as if he had never been exposed to death. Both of his parents had died, one of his sisters had died in her thirties, and he had lost a few friends at work. Each of these deaths had left him sad, but they never gave him pause to consider his own mortality.

But things were different now. He told me it was as if someone had flipped a light switch in his mind, and he could now see everything far more clearly than he ever could before. He certainly had many happy memories and like everyone else, he harbored a few significant regrets. But what was nagging at him was the realization that he had never paid any attention to what he now called "The Big Picture." Because of this, he now bore the burden of knowing he had missed out on living a life that was truly meaningful.

We shared many things as we talked that day. Jeff's eyes had certainly been opened. Perhaps the saddest comment he made that day was that though he wanted to talk to his grandchildren about his discovery and to give them a warning not to make the same mistake that he had, he told me that he wouldn't because "this is not how they know me."

At his funeral, everyone talked about what a great guy Jeff was. I found myself mourning his death in a different way. When someone young dies, we mourn that they never had a chance to really live, implying that if they had only had the chance for a full life then their death would not be so hard to take. I mourned Jeff's death because he died with the nagging sense that he had wasted his time on earth. Though he had lived for sixty-nine years and had lots of chances to explore, discover, grow, and live, he never did. Perhaps the greatest tragedy was that even though he finally realized it, by then it was too late to do anything about it. Jeff died, but he apparently never fully lived. Helen Keller wrote, "Life is either a daring adventure, or nothing" (17). Jeff came too late to the tragic conclusion that his life had not been a daring adventure.

Everyone dies. Of that there can be no doubt. Despite trillions of dollars spent every year on medical care and enormous efforts (at least by some) at eating well, exercising, and getting enough rest, everyone ends up at the same place. Dead. Death is unavoidable, but life is a choice. The real question worth considering is whether everyone actually lives before they die. But what defines truly living? Does a beating heart mean you are really alive? Does holding down a steady job qualify? Does being married and having children count as a full life? Is life a matter of keeping your head down, your blinders on, and plodding along the trail of days, like a plough horse, according to the dictates of the calendar? Does life become more meaningful when we add more to the schedule and increase the pace? In the end, it all becomes a question of "what is life?"

What is life? That is a silly question! The answer should be easy. How can something as basic as life be so vexing? Hasn't there been anyone smart enough to figure it out and reduce it to an elegant equation where we can tweak the variables and produce varied, but expected outcomes? But, of course, it is not an easy question. Interestingly, this struggle is a uniquely human dilemma. After all, a lion does not need to learn how to be a lion. It just is. A dog does not need to learn how to be a dog. It just is. Lions do not question the morality of killing and eating a baby zebra; they just do it. Dogs do not debate whether or not their loyalty to their owners is earning them the proper rewards; they are just loyal. But human beings have always struggled with the fundamental question of what it means to be fully human. It is as if we have lost our instinctual understanding of ourselves. We have lost a core knowledge that theologians, philosophers, and scientists have spent the last few thousand years trying to recover.

Western civilization has wrestled seriously with the meaning of life since before the time of the ancient Greek philosophers 2,500 years ago. In *The Republic*, Plato gives his famous example of people growing up living in a cave where they can only see the back wall and shadows cast on it by people moving by at the front of the cave. Because the shadows are all the people ever see, they then conclude that the shadows are reality. Plato saw most people as living this way. Their understanding of life was limited just to what they could see and the task of philosophers was to lead them to the entrance of the cave where they could see real people and the light of the sun itself. Though this would be a difficult and unpleasant experience for the newly liberated people, they would quickly adjust and then live in a world in which they have a much better understanding of what is real and what is merely shadow. For Plato, it was only when you knew this difference that you could truly be alive in a meaningful way.

Other attempts to address these questions included the Greek philosophical school whose students were known as Epicureans, who sought to focus on the "here and now," and pursued a life of modest means that focused on experiencing pleasure and avoiding pain. They saw little value in focusing on ephemeral or mystical questions and were very pragmatic. For them, the goal of life was to have fun. Another group, the Stoics, sought to live lives based on self-control and the curbing of emotions that could quickly spiral out of control. Clear thinking and emotional detachment from life were the highest goals. Stoics believed that if they had a rational enough understanding of life, then no emotional shock could dislodge it. A third group, known as the Cynics, sought to abandon the trappings of civilization altogether and to live as close to nature as possible. Wealth, fame, and power were all seen as artificial and as pursuits that would only lead to suffering. True happiness, they argued, came from simplicity and self-sufficiency. Not only did they pursue this, but they also felt compelled to point out the follies and useless pursuits of others in society. Each of these schools had their followers and there are many today who still follow the tenets of one or more of these schools, perhaps even without knowing it.

Since the dawn of the Scientific Revolution in the sixteenth century, the focus has been on science and its perceived abilities to solve (eventually) all the problems of life. Advances in chemistry led to the belief that our quality of life would inevitably improve, advances in medicine led to the belief that we would eventually end all suffering, and advances in transportation led to the belief that the world was coming together and that mobility would bring complete freedom. We are also rapidly gaining an understanding of how the physical universe works. We understand everything from the characteristics of quarks to the movement of galaxies. We can build two-thousand-foot-tall skyscrapers and manipulate individual atoms. The scientific advances are occurring at a breathtaking pace, and many people today put their hope in science and progress. But science is still unable to define such basic human traits as faith, love, beauty, mortality, and holiness (all uniquely human qualities). It is interesting to note that there is still no scientific explanation as to why music has the effect it does on people. We are the only species on the plant to have developed musical instruments, yet every human civilization that has existed has done so. Perhaps the Austrian-British philosopher, Ludwig Wittgenstein, got it right. He argued that even when all of the scientific questions have been addressed, science will have still left untouched the main problems of life. Advances in technology can make life more convenient, but not more meaningful. The reason for this is that science has tended to focus on questions of "how" rather than on the deeper questions of "why."

It has only been in the last generation or so that people have seriously begun to question their faith in the scientific method. Two of the issues that have come to the forefront are the issue of the false dualisms that we have inherited from the ancient Greeks and the failure of the effects of all scientific progress to be positive. Greek philosophy included a number of dualisms, and inevitably, one part of the dualism was seen as more valuable than the other part. Distinctions were made between intellect and emotion, between faith and reason, between soul and body, and between male and female. You can imagine which side of each dualism has been seen as more important and more valuable in Western civilization. In recent years, we have come to see that these are false choices. A well-balanced person does not choose reason over faith, intellect over emotion, and soul over body anymore. We have also finally come to recognize the equality and complementarity of the sexes, instead of forcing a superior vs. inferior dynamic. We see that there is the need to balance both parts of each dualism. Also the belief that all scientific discoveries and all technological progress is good seems almost naïve in a nuclear armed, polluted, and still wildly violent world. For each problem that technology solves, it creates a new one. Any good use of technology tends to have an equally bad use. For many philosophers, the golden age of reason (called the Enlightenment) came to an inglorious end in 1914 when the "war to end all wars" (World War I) used a number of new technologies (submarines, airplanes, poison gas, and armored tanks) to introduce killing on an industrial scale.

So where does this leave us today?

Some people are fatalistic. They see life as being beyond their ability to influence, and so they see little meaning or purpose in wrestling with it. The story is told of a man once being asked by a passing reporter what kind of project he was working on in the middle of the city street. The reporter thought it was some sort of repair, but the response he received was far more philosophical: "I dig the ditch to earn the money to buy the food to gain the strength to dig the ditch." This worker was someone who had a completely fatalistic view of life and saw neither hope nor growth in his life. His work served no other purpose than to provide the food to enable more work.

Some people tend to be cynical. They see others working harder and harder without making any progress. They see most people as having bought into the idea that having more stuff will make them happy, working as hard as they can to get more stuff. However, the efforts of these other people at work and at accumulating more stuff leads to exhaustion long before it brings happiness. For cynics, this is all a waste of time. An apt motto for them is a variation of the old bumper sticker that says, "The one who dies with the most toys wins." But in their variation, it says, "The one who dies with the most toys is still dead."

Some people continue to put their hope in science. They believe that because we have equations that show an orderly universe, life can be properly ordered and understood. Along with this is usually the belief that because of the technological progress science has created, science will one day fix all of the problems or struggles we have today. Their vision is akin to the one portrayed in the original *Star Trek* series on television. It is a society where everyone strives to be their best for purely altruistic motives, and money no longer exists because people are no longer materialistic or motivated by monetary gain. It is an idealistic and utopian world that does not honestly recognize the failings of human nature.

Though academics do have the time and leisure to debate the finer points of philosophy and life, it seems that for the rest of us, the focus stays more on the here and now. After all, how can one wrestle with whether or not life has a specific purpose when they are focused on not being late for the next appointment, trying to remember to get the oil in the car changed, needing to return a library book, having to get the laundry done so the children will have clean socks, needing to make an appointment with the veterinarian, and on and on? It is what some call "the Tyranny of the Immediate." Everything that doesn't have an immediate deadline is pushed to the back burner, and it is always going to be very hard to view the Big Picture as a priority in the midst of the Tyranny of the Immediate. Given the pressures of daily life, it is easy to see why this is so. Many of us are just barely able to keep up with it all, and nothing, except for perhaps our own imminent death, ever compels the questions related to the Big Picture to come to the forefront. Life can get lost in the details of living.

However, are we really this busy, or do we make ourselves busy? Are 100 percent of our minds occupied 100 percent of the time, or do we subconsciously choose to fill every moment with noise so that we don't have to let our minds wander to scary topics related to the Big Picture? Think about the distractive technologies you use every day. Many people have radios playing as they shower in the morning, watch television as they eat breakfast, play their radio in the car (or the MP3 player while on the train or bus), have background music at work, and put the television back on from the moment they get home until bedtime (that is, unless they're playing computer games or surfing the Internet). There is not a single moment of quiet or silent time in the course of the entire day! Family therapists bemoan the fact that too many families eat dinner in front of the TV instead of at a table together. It seems that it is easier to sit passively and be entertained by television than it is to do the work of relationships. Is all this noise really necessary, or is some of it merely being used for distraction?

In his search for personal and spiritual meaning, Henry David Thoreau wrote in *Walden* more than a hundred years ago, "The mass of men lead lives of quiet desperation. . . . A stereotyped but unconscious despair is concealed even under what are called the games and amusements of mankind" (8). Thoreau believed that most people knew their lives lacked the meaning or purpose that would bring happiness and that even their "games and amusements" could not hide that fact. His book was an exploration into what it means to be truly alive and how to "suck out all the marrow of life" (118). To do this, he lived a semi-reclusive life for more than two years, and at the end, he concluded that it is destructive to the soul to conform to the norms and values of society. For Thoreau, the highest good was for each person to fight against the distractions and to find his or her own path through life. Yet, even in finding one's path through life, there was still the sense that we are each alone.

If we use daily life to escape from the questions of life and fill every moment with noise, what is it we are trying to escape from? What is it we are afraid of? For some, the fear is nihilism, the fear that in the final analysis, life is meaningless. Nihilistic belief holds that humans evolved accidentally, make their way through their days without any higher purpose, and then cease to exist after death. Nihilists tend to be very depressed by nature and the best example of it in society today is in some of the music. Among many nihilists there is a sense of, "life sucks, then you die."

Others resist questions of life and meaning because there is a fear that by admitting the existence of God, one must also admit there are obligations to be fulfilled. Some picture the extreme of being obligated to be dour, rule-bound, joyless, and avoiding frivolity at all costs. It is as if that by admitting that God exists, we must give up who we are and adhere to a harsh and rigid lifestyle. And, of course, this is all liberally sprinkled with a heavy dose of guilt! For these folks, there is a quiet belief that "ignorance is bliss," and since the answer is probably not the one you want, it is better not to ask the question in the first place.

Still others believe that we can only be happy when we are free from responsibilities, obligations, and commitments. This is the hedonistic approach exemplified by the American advertising industry, which would have you believe that freedom is the only truth. In this view, you can only be happy when you are young, rich, famous, and sexually satisfied. Consumption is the only true good in life and meaning can only be found when you are free from responsibilities that would "tie you down" and in possession of the latest and hippest fashions, toys, and gadgets. These are the people who believe they will only be able to say they had a good life if, at the end of it, they are able to say they did what they wanted, when they wanted, because it made them feel good at the time.

All these approaches are wrong. They are not based in reality. Nihilism is fatalistic and depressing. Guilt-driven obedience is a cartoonish stereotype of religion that few actually would even begin to believe in. Total freedom is empty. We know that children develop better when they are raised in the context of structure and boundaries than when they are free to do whatever they want. The same is true for adults. Hedonism has led to a culture that is medicated for depression, in therapy, and alone. All these options come up short. Contrast this with people who are happy, serene, and very good at what they do. These are people who have a keen sense of why they are alive and what they should be doing. They know that true happiness comes from understanding why we are alive, knowing what our purpose in life is, and in living within its structure. They will not experience the regrets about ignoring the Big Picture in their lives that Jeff knew in his.

Take a moment to reflect on your own life. What do you think the true meaning of life is? Do you merely focus on getting through today without much regard for the trajectory of your life or what is going to happen long term? Do you focus on escapism just to pass the time, focusing your attention and giving all your available energy to a particular hobby, sport, gambling, drinking, drugs, or television? Each one of these is a way to either forget about the responsibilities and challenges of life or a means of living vicariously through others. In moderation, most of these are mere entertainment and can serve as a wonderful release. It is when they become all-consuming that they turn into an escape. Sadly, many people get caught up in escapism and end up sleepwalking through real life. They are physically present, but they are contributing and accomplishing little. There is a sports radio station in Boston that for a time referred to some of its listeners as "blood thirsty shut-ins." These tend to be people who are caught up in escapism and try to live vicariously through one of the four major sports teams in the city. When their favorite team fails to live up to their expectations, they respond with outrage and a personal sense of betrayal. They vent their anger on the airwaves of the radio station. These are people who have a poor sense of balance because they rely on sports teams to provide real meaning for their lives, something that entertainment can never live up to. While venting their anger at the host, they do not see how they are being made fun of for not having a healthy perspective on life.

The Christian definition of the meaning of life is fairly different and more straightforward, wherein humans exist in order to love and serve God. Key to this definition are the ideas that humans are made in God's image (Creation), creation is broken (the Fall), God offers a way back from the wilderness (the Atonement), making that journey requires a conscious decision (conversion), and life is lived in the context of this pilgrimage (sanctification). Let's look at each of these points individually.

The beginning of Christian teaching is that God created humanity to be in relationship with him. To say that humans were created in God's image means that when we see one another, we are to see the reflection of God. By extension, this means that we should view and love everyone as we view and love God. This is the source of the Christian emphasis on charity and aid for the poor, the sick, and the outcast, which is manifested in so many ways: building orphanages, building hospitals, developing prison ministries, staffing homeless shelters, working with community aid agencies, and addressing the great moral questions that our society wrestles with today. By seeing Jesus in the people who are served, Christians live up to Jesus' reminder, "Whatever you did for one of the least of these brothers and sisters of mine, you did for me" (Matt. 25:40). We cannot see other people as a means to serve our own ends, as our self-absorbed culture encourages us to. We must see them as holy creations of God.

Though God looked upon creation at the beginning and said, "It is good," we know that creation is broken. We do not live to our fullest potential, as life is saturated with suffering, hatred, and violence. The Fall means that we have lost the ability to see the image of God in each other and have instead been reduced to looking only for gain for ourselves. The meaning of the Garden of Eden story is that when given the choice between living in paradise on God's terms, or living in a broken and hurting world on our own terms, we chose to live on our own terms. The Original Sin is the human desire to have power and control over the universe, rather than to live in harmony under God's authority. This conflict is represented by the lie the serpent told Eve in the Garden of Eden. What convinced her to eat the forbidden fruit was the idea that she could "be like God." It would be a mistake to think that this story is just about the sin of Adam and Eve. (If this were so, then the debate about whether the Garden of Eden actually existed would be a more important one.) This is not just about Adam and Eve; it is a parable of human nature. The mistake of Adam and Eve is the same mistake that each and every one of us makes in our own lives. The world we have built is one of competing interests, exploitation, and mercilessness.

Other people are often seen as serving a means to our own ends. We tend to focus our attention on our own needs and wants. When we do this, our focus is not on God, which means that our relationship with God is broken, which is to say that we have "fallen" from the place of grace we were supposed to live in.

Given that we have chosen to follow our own paths, we might easily understand why God would choose to walk away from the whole mess. What better lesson would there be for humans than to be left to live with the consequences of their own folly? But that's not what happens. Another key teaching of Christianity is forgiveness. God doesn't give up, but instead offers forgiveness and shows humanity how to come back in from the wilderness. This is done through the life and work of Jesus. The idea that God would become a human being is hard for many to understand. Why would God choose to do this? Not only so God could *tell* us how to live, but so that God could *show* us how to live. Jesus' life and teaching represents a powerful lesson on how life can overcome death, how love can overcome hate, and how God is willing to solve the problem of sin for all time.

The death of Jesus on the cross is an essential component of his mission. In the Old Testament, the religious life of the people revolved around the activities of the Temple in Jerusalem. Jews from all over the known world would travel to Jerusalem to make sacrificial offerings to God. In sacrificing something of their own (usually a lamb), the people would show remorse for their sin and would promise to live their lives in a more holy way. The most important religious holiday of the year was the Day of Atonement (Yom Kippur), on which the high priest would enter the Holy of Holies and sprinkle the blood of a sacrificial lamb to atone for the sins of the whole nation.

In the crucifixion of Jesus, we see the sacrificial "Lamb of God, who takes away the sin of the world" (John 1:29) sacrificed for all of humanity. In his death, all of the sins of the world are atoned for, and this act is not something that will need to be repeated over and over; it was accomplished once, for all time. It shows the extent God will go to in order to restore the broken relationship with humanity. As Jesus said, "Greater love has no one than this: to lay down one's life for one's friends" (John 15:13). In his death on the cross, we see these words in action.

As with the giving of any gift, there were two parts to this one. The first occurs when the giver gives the gift. The second part takes place when the receiver decides whether or not to accept it. If the receiver accepts the gift, then he or she gets to enjoy the full benefit of it. If the receiver does not accept the gift, they cannot benefit from it. After all, if my brother offered me a new computer game and I responded with, "no thanks," should I then later complain that I do not get to play with the game? That would be silly. Likewise, if we seek to benefit from the Atonement and from God's offer of forgiveness, then we must accept it. How do we do that? This is the moment of conversion. At some point, each of us must have that moment where we make a conscious decision to accept God's gift. For some people, this is a very clear moment, and they can name the day and time when it happened. For others, it is part of a long and slow process of growth and reflection. In either case, there must at some point be the conscious decision to accept it . . . and the responsibility that goes with it. What is that responsibility? If the Fall happened because we chose to follow our own path in life over God's, then the Restoration means that we change direction and choose to follow God's path in life over our own.

This decision to follow God is not a small one. It is a full surrender, and it is a complete commitment. This isn't about deciding to hang out with a friend for the evening; this is committing to a marriage. Once the commitment is made, the journey that follows is referred to by academics as the process of sanctification, but it is also called the process of discipleship (the word "disciple" comes from a Latin word that means learner or student). This journey is one that takes a lifetime. It will have ups and downs, happiness and sadness, victories and defeats, and good times and bad times. However, during this journey, you learn how to see the world as God sees it, you learn how to love others as God loves them, you learn how to live as God wants you to live, and you come to understand the true meaning of life. It is a hard journey, but it is the only path to serenity and inner peace. It is the only path that fully lives life in the context of the big picture, because it is the only path that seeks to understand life the way God understands life. It is also the only path that seeks to live life the way God desires for us to live.

This means that holiness is not separate from the struggles and challenges of daily life; instead, it is found in the midst of them. To truly live is to see the holy and to experience the holy even in the midst of what many consider to be the routine and the ordinary. In the remainder of this book, we will look at how to develop a Christian worldview; how to hear the voice of God when you pray; how we undertake the journey into living a whole life; how we learn what spiritual disciplines aid in our pilgrimage on earth, what a Rule for Life is, and what it means to live in the incubator of wholeness; how to define our lives; how to set meaningful long term goals; and how to deal with life when things go wrong. The goal of this book is to help you go through this process so you can then create your own Rule for Life that will govern your pilgrimage.

As Helen Keller wrote, "Life is either a daring adventure, or nothing." We have all seen what it is like to live a life that is nothing. Let us embark on the daring adventure that leads to true life!

2

Worldviews

*"If you don't know where you're going,
any road will take you there."*

—George Harrison, "Any Road"

Have you ever heard the phrase, "Seeing is believing"? The idea is that if you cannot see it, then it cannot be real. If someone tells you that they have completed a major renovation project on their house, you may be doubtful if this person has a history of "embellishing" their accomplishments. The only way to ensure that they are describing what they have actually done is to see the completed work for yourself. This sounds like an objective way to look at life, but is it? If we are doubtful of the skills of the person, will we only notice their mistakes or shortcuts? If we hold the person in very high regard, will we miss the mistakes and only see a magnificent project carried

31

to perfection? While seeing *is* believing, the problem is that we often only see what we want to see, and we completely miss what we want to miss. We have preconceived notions about the world, about people, about life, and about God, and what we see often is meant to do little more than reinforce those understandings. This chapter will help you to understand why.

The Human Brain

The complexity of the human brain is staggering. Though it weighs around three pounds and makes up only 2 percent of the total weight of the human body, it can consume up to 25 percent of the energy the body uses! There are as many as one hundred billion neurons and as many as a quadrillion synaptic connections. New knowledge or the development of new skills leads to a physical restructuring of the neural pathways, and neglected knowledge or skills lead to the atrophy or even dissolution of other pathways. During waking hours, the brain regulates body functions, reacts to external stimuli, and engages in a constant process of cognitive processing. During sleep, the brain continues to regulate body functions, and it also engages in a process of sorting and storing the experiences of the day.

Given this degree of complexity, it is important that the brain organize, sort, and prioritize the many processes that it must engage in so that it can function effectively. The number of thoughts required to fully function would quickly overwhelm the capacity of our conscious thought processes, so the brain works to "automate" as many functions as possible, which allows it to focus more energy on items that require more detailed conscious thought. The brain stem automates basic bodily functioning like the heart rate, digestion, temperature control, breathing, blinking, and more so the body can function at healthy levels. All this takes place at a totally unconscious level. The brain also automates highly routine or repetitive functions. Skills that can require considerable effort to learn can eventually become automated enough to not disturb the conscious thought processes. For example, young people learning how to shave are completely focused on the task for fear of cutting themselves. An adult with many years of shaving experience will give little conscious thought to the process. Learning to drive a car can be a harrowing experience for a teenager, yet an experienced driver can give her attention to multiple other tasks while driving and do so successfully (usually).

Not only does the brain automate basic and routine functions, it also serves as a filter for information. If we hear a loud and unfamiliar noise in the sky, we will immediately pay attention. However, if an airplane is flying by, there is a good chance we will not even notice. The sound of the plane is routine and familiar to the brain, so it elicits little reaction and is filtered out. Another example: You can drive for an hour and not really notice any of the cars you pass going in the other direction. However, if you become really interested in a particular model and are considering buying one, you will suddenly notice every one that you pass. In this case, your brain has decided to turn off the filtering in order to draw attention to that specific model of car.

Worldview

Another process the brain engages in is that it constructs an understanding of life and of the world and will process all experiences and stimuli through the lens of that perspective. These perspectives, our worldviews, function automatically. We do not consciously form them, process information with them, reflect on them, or even question them. They are part of the wiring in our brains that allows us to see things as we already assume them to be. Information that is consistent with our worldviews is accepted, while information that contradicts them is discarded without much conscious awareness that this is happening.

Just as a pair of glasses will filter what our eyes see without our giving thought to the process, our worldviews will filter how we perceive and understand any given situation or experience. Glasses function to help us. Worldviews, though, work not to improve perception, but to instead make understanding cognitive inputs easier and quicker, even if that apparent efficiency produces objectively inaccurate results.

To put things more formally, a worldview is a fundamental set of assumptions and beliefs about how the world works and about how life is supposed to be perceived and lived. A person's worldview defines how she or he perceives reality. Its construction is based on experiences, education, lessons learned, and socialization into a particular culture. When people interpret sensory stimuli, experiences, or memories, they understand those things in the context of their worldview. In other words, we do not see the world as it is; we see the world as we are.

The development of a worldview is usually an automatic and mostly unconscious process that can only be restructured with great intentional effort. A worldview can hold morally desirable or morally repugnant values—or even both types of values simultaneously—while defining a host of things: what is good, what is evil, what is fair, what is just, what can be accepted, what must be fought, who can be trusted, and what really matters in life. As part of their worldview, a person can have the belief that most people should be trusted, but can also believe in certain negative racial stereotypes. A worldview can also perpetuate poor behaviors that resulted from emotional stress or trauma. Social fads and fashions often play an important role in a person's choosing which values to either follow or resist. Unhealthy clinical conditions, like codependency, depression, the generational effects of alcoholism, and a host of others, can also be woven into one's worldview. Those who are "slaves to fashion" have a worldview that includes the belief that having the latest "in" things makes them better people. This conviction serves as a motivation to work hard to stay current. Interestingly, a similar motivation can drive a religious person to engage in more prayer time, more worship attendance, and more spiritually related activities. The drive and energy are the same, but put to very different uses in an attempt to accomplish the same goal: being a better person. The only difference is the worldview through which "being a better person" is defined. This example illustrates the power that a worldview can exert on a person.

Worldviews are also shaped by education, family background, experiences, role models, personal biases, prejudices, goals, self-image, influences, habits, hobbies, favorite books, television programs, radio programs, movies, and music. All of these experiences, and the thoughts and habits related to them, combine in a unique way for each individual. Whereas one person will be strongly influenced by patterns learned from her parents (perhaps to the point where she uses the same phrases and vocal inflections as her mother), another will be strongly influenced by a movie (just think of obsessive *Star Wars* or *Lord of the Rings* fans).

With a particular worldview in place, when an individual encounters an experience, the worldview will strongly influence how the person understands and deals with that experience. If a person who is a racist hears that an individual of whatever race they look down on has done something bad, the racist worldview will automatically confirm it as further evidence for the justification of the racism, saying, "Of course, that's what they all do." However, if someone of the disrespected race does something noble, shows brilliance, or exhibits a behavior that is counterintuitive for the racist person hearing about it, the racist worldview will likely dismiss the example as being irrelevant and will quickly put it aside. Later, the racist may not even remember what they saw. This, in part, is why it is so hard to have reasonable discussions about prejudices and biases. These can tend to be so embedded in a person's worldview that the individual just assumes them to be true. Since the person cannot contextualize a scenario where their beliefs would be seen to be wrong, any discussion about the possibilities of being wrong tends to be futile.

This knowledge of bias is why Jesus' parable of the Good Samaritan in the Gospel of Luke is such a compelling story. In first-century Israel, Jews almost universally hated Samaritans, who were Jews who had intermarried pagans after the fall of the northern kingdom of Israel in 722 BC. By the first century AD, their descendants had developed cultural and religious differences that made them even more despised than the Roman Empire. They were seen as half-breeds, and the abhorrence toward them was so severe that a Jew traveling from Galilee in the north of Israel to Jerusalem in the south would make a significant detour to the east through Syria, rather than travel due south and pass through Samaritan territory. Even though they were closely related by ethnic background, history, and religion, most Jews saw their differences as being significant enough to think of Samaritans as being no better than traitors.

Jesus tells the parable of the Good Samaritan while he is teaching a Jewish crowd and arguing that we must love our neighbor as ourselves. Someone in the crowd asks who our neighbor is. His response to the question is to tell a story of a Jew who was robbed, beaten, and left in a ditch. A Levite (a religious leader) went by and ignored the man. Then a priest (an even more important holy person) also went by, and also left the man lying in the ditch. Finally, a Samaritan came by, helped the man, and went the extra mile in bringing him to an inn and ensuring his continued care. To a Jewish audience hearing this story, it would have been deeply troubling, because it would have gone completely against their worldview in which Samaritans were wretched and neither deserved help nor were expected to do good deeds for Jews. If his hearers were to take this lesson seriously, they would need to conclude that if they were to honestly love their neighbors, then they must love those they have always seen as their worst enemies. Such a shift cannot take place without a significant change in worldview, one that redefines the nature of how others are seen and how others are to be treated. I suspect that most of his hearers did not let the story get past their worldviews, and so they concluded that he was offensive and wrong in his teaching. Doing so allowed them to maintain their worldview and dismiss the parable. It also allowed them to develop a hatred for Jesus that later played out in the enthusiastic reactions of the crowd on Good Friday when they heard he was to be crucified.

If you would like to test your own response to the parable, think for a minute about a group, race, culture, political party, denomination, religion, nation, neighbor, or even relative that you just cannot stand. This only works if you are really honest with yourself and are willing to name who it is you do not like or who drives you crazy. You might be tempted to dismiss this question by saying you love everyone, but since such a reality is rather unlikely, you need to be able to name your true attitudes. Can you be that honest? Can you name a person or group? If so, then imagine them as the hero of the parable. What are your feelings related to that idea? What do you do with those feelings?

Chuck Colson, in his book *How Now Shall We Live?* argues that our individual worldviews are defined by how we each answer a series of questions:

- Where do we come from, and who are we (a question of creation)?
- What has gone wrong with the world (how did the world become fallen)?
- What can we do to fix it (the question of redemption)? (14)

He argues that our understanding of the nature and purpose of creation, our understanding of why the world functions so poorly and our understanding of how we can restore that which has been lost will define everything else about how we see, understand, and live life.

In other words, people who see their origin as meaningful and purposeful are more likely to have a positive outlook on life than people who see everything as accidental and pointless. Likewise, people with a positive image of the future will likely do more to help bring that future about than those who have no hope and see only death at the end of life. Our worldviews can determine our levels of commitment to or our engagement with the world. One person may be highly energized by and deeply committed to the eradication of homelessness, while another person may exhibit a similar passion for maintaining physical health, while still a third will exhibit a passion for model railroading. In each case, the individual will have drawn different conclusions based on a host of factors enmeshed in their worldview and will then act accordingly. And, all the while, they will be bemused and mystified as to why others have chosen to follow a different path!

Worldview is tricky because so much of it develops unconsciously. In the story of *Snow White and the Seven Dwarfs,* whenever the queen asked the mirror on the wall who was the fairest, she only wanted to hear the mirror say that she was the most beautiful, and she grew very angry when the mirror did not accommodate her. Our worldview can act like an accommodating mirror. It can tell us what we want to hear, show us the world the way we want to see it, and leave us feeling like our accomplishments are grand and our sins are trivial. It accomplishes this in part by filtering out information that contradicts its self-understanding. Facts, experiences, or ideas that contradict a particular worldview pass through the brain without stopping and without leaving any traces of having been there. The brain is not being nefarious but rather is maintaining equilibrium in order to function efficiently and reserve cognitive capacity to process other information. In other words, it serves as a shortcut that frees the brain from having to do extra work reframing its whole understanding of life every time a new bit of information is added to the database.

It is important not to underestimate the significance of worldview. It not only reinforces our perspective on life, but it can influence the limits of our endurance. In *Why Do Bad Things Happen to Good People?* Melvin Tinker cites Friedrich Nietzsche as saying, "Men and women can endure any amount of suffering so long as they know the why to their existence" (23). If there is a clear definition as to why someone exists, that why can bolster the person's endurance to overcome any travail or hardship. One's worldview defines the why of existence. During World War II, Viktor Frankl, a Jewish psychiatrist from Germany, was sent to a concentration camp. He survived the ordeal and later wrote *Man's Search for Meaning,* in which he shared how he learned in the concentration camp that inmates spared from the gas chambers did not die or survive based on their physical strength or stamina. Given that their days were spent toiling in heavy labor, with little food, and constant physical abuse, it seems fair to assume that physical stamina would be the primary determining factor in survival. Instead, Frankl observed, people tended to live or die based on whether they had a purpose for living that overrode their fear of death in the concentration camp. Frankl wrote of many instances where frail people who had the will to live outlasted very strong people who did not.

The process of filtering out information is not always systematic or consistently logical. When a person holds mutually contradictory views, their mind may try to rationalize the contradiction despite the cognitive dissonance. A great example is that though most people reject the notion that psychics have any actual power, they are also aware that police departments sometimes use them in missing persons and other types of cases. Another example would be that though most people reject the notion that a full moon causes people to behave oddly, many know people in the medical profession who tell them that emergency rooms get unusually busy when the moon is full. A third example would be the practice of dowsing, the use of divining rods to find underground water or pipes. Though most people see this practice as silly, I have seen them used more than once (it is quite a sight to see several construction workers and a number of pieces of large equipment waiting while a dowser finds the pipe they need to dig up!). Much more routine examples can occur as well. For example, a spendthrift can be perfectly aware of the importance of the need to save money and of avoiding excessive debt, but at the same time carry credit card debts in excess of fifty thousand dollars, and many people gamble in casinos knowing full well the house always wins in the end. When people hold on to particular ideas despite all evidence to the contrary, their worldview is trumping their cognitive thought processes—they can think that they are thinking or behaving rationally and have no idea just how wrong they are.

Worldviews can also be damaged. A traumatic experience can lead to extreme consequences. The medical condition known as post-traumatic stress disorder (PTSD) occurs to combat veterans, emergency service workers, and disaster survivors when they are exposed to a traumatic shock that so affronts and damages their worldviews that they become unable to process the experience in any meaningful way. The trauma in effect short circuits the brain's normal functioning and creates a host of physiological and psychological problems. For example, an individual who always assumed that the world was a safe place and that their home would always be secure can have their worldview shattered by a natural disaster. If in a single unforeseen incident the person loses her home, all of her possessions, and witnesses the death of a loved one, she is usually unable to process this reality through her worldview. This inability to bring the new reality through the filters of the worldview causes a short circuit in the disaster survivor's brain and leads the person to exhibit diminished cognitive capacity (to the point where they appear to be moving in slow motion), frenetic behavior, extreme hostility, obsessive-compulsive behavior, or a host of other behaviors. The effects of PTSD cannot be undone until the sufferer is able to reconstruct her worldview in a manner that incorporates and contextualizes the horrific experience that has been endured. This work of contextualization cannot be completed by the individual in isolation. It usually requires a lot of work with a trained therapist.

This is the power of worldviews. We shape them, often unintentionally, and then they shape us for the rest of our lives. They can determine how we see life, and when they are threatened, they can seriously impair our cognitive abilities. We need to understand them, because if we seek to change direction in life, we first need to know what governs the direction we are already traveling in. As George Harrison sang, "If you don't know where you're going, any road will take you there." To truly live, you must know where you are going! To go where you desire, you must properly orient your worldview in that direction. Developing a specifically Christian worldview is important because we want even our subconscious and unconscious decisions to be consistent with God's will for the desires and actions of our lives.

Despite the seeming permanence of worldviews, they are actually somewhat malleable. A key argument of this book is that, with effort and through the development of a Rule for Life that we follow with discipline and consistency, we can shape and redefine our worldviews—and if we truly wish to fully live before we die, we need to work to develop a worldview that is consistent with a Christian understanding of the nature of life and why God set this universe up in the manner that he did.

Worldview Examples

In earlier times, worldviews were rarely articulated because limitations on travel kept people in a community where most everyone shared the same worldview. It was an unconscious part of community life that few ever reflected upon. People were not seen so much as individual persons as they were seen as being part of the tribe or clan. It has only been in more recent generations, where international travel has become commonplace and developments have been made in understanding how the brain works, that people have recognized the existence of many different worldviews and have begun to address them.

Though there can be as many specific worldviews as there are people, there are certain general overarching models within which most people will develop their worldviews, and these are models that tend to be easily recognized. In Chapter One, we met Jeff, a man who had never thought about the meaning of life until it was time to die. His worldview was rather basic, and one that is common. He had few expectations from life. He sought to be comfortable and to educate his children. His joy came from golfing or in spending time on his small sailboat. His worldview was one that had little perspective on time. He did not plan much for the future, and he did not see his own life as having any purpose other than to provide for his children. His only career goal was to remain with the utility company he was working for until retirement, and he believed that they would provide a pension that would keep him comfortable in his old age. He believed in God, but his understanding of heaven had not progressed from the understanding he had learned in the second grade of Sunday school (his last year of formal, church-based education). To Jeff, one went to heaven for being a decent person. His worldview did not reflect on the past or contemplate the future. His focus was to work today and to look forward to the weekend.

Another example of a specific worldview is held by practitioners of Buddhism. They believe that life is governed by the law of karma. Karma is the belief that all of one's thoughts and actions in this life will be added up at death and the individual will be reincarnated into a new body based on karma. If your good karma outweighs your bad karma, then you will come back in a better form—perhaps into a wealthier family, a more peaceful nation, or with more abilities. If your bad karma outweighs your good, then you will come back in a worse form—perhaps into a country at war, into poverty, with a physical handicap, or as an animal. Karma also teaches that we begin our state in each life based on our actions in our last life, and our motivation for doing good comes from wanting to come back better in the next life. The way to assuage guilt is to believe that even if you don't get it fully right in this life, if you at least live a decent life, then you won't be any worse off in the next one and will be able to try again. The ultimate goal for Buddhists is Nirvana, which is seen as the end of existence for the soul, a desirable thing because reaching it will stop the cycle of reincarnations into a world full of suffering.

Buddhism is a non-theistic religion and does not have a deity (a god or gods) as the focus of devotion. It refuses to speculate much on the unseen reality, since it holds that we cannot really know such things. Speculation about the unknown is seen as a distraction from what must be done in the here and now. Buddhists also see this world as an illusion and a mere distraction from spiritual growth, because attachment to anything in this world can only lead to suffering. The Four Noble Truths and the Eightfold Path that define Buddhist thought are meant to help followers detach themselves, to remove themselves from having any love for or sense of attachment to anything or anyone. Achieving complete detachment from everything opens the door to Nirvana.

The Four Noble Truths are: (1) life is suffering; (2) attachment to things, people, or even ideas is the cause of suffering; (3) one's goal must be to pursue the end of suffering; and (4) following the Eightfold Path leads to the end of suffering. The life of a Buddhist is spent pursuing the Eightfold Path, which is: (1) Right View (seeing the world as it really is); (2) Right Intention (having the resolve to follow the correct path); (3) Right Speech (being honest and having integrity in our dealings with others); (4) Right Action (behaving honorably); (5) Right Livelihood (having a career that does not involve hurting others); (6) Right Effort (working to eliminate all bad thoughts, words, and actions); (7) Right Mindfulness (being always aware of surroundings and reactions to phenomena); and (8) Right Concentration (learning how to completely focus).

To live within a Buddhist worldview, one must concentrate at all times on what will contribute to developing a sense of detachment and avoiding what will only distract the practitioner from becoming detached. No thought, experience, or idea is neutral. Every moment of every day brings the person closer to, or drives him farther away from, the goal.

Every experience, every encounter with anyone, and every thought must be filtered through the worldview to decide if it contributes to good or bad karma. Over time, devout Buddhists develop a worldview wherein everything deemed to contribute to negative karma is automatically discarded so that people can focus only on experiences that add to good karma. This focus on goodness is what gives advanced practitioners such a sense of equanimity.

Western civilization has followed a very different worldview for the better part of the last three hundred years, most often attributed to the Enlightenment, or Modernity. This dramatic shift in perspective arose in the late seventeenth century and sought to replace what many at the time saw as the superstition of medieval Europe with a focus on science and reason. Building on the Scientific Revolution that began in the sixteenth century, the political revolutions in the eighteenth century (centering in the United States and France), and the Industrial Revolution beginning in the early nineteenth century, Enlightenment thinkers believed that science and reason needed to replace the religious mysticism of medievalism. Along with the rapid progress of science and industrialization came the belief that life was on an inevitable and always upward track; that science and technology were inherently good and were eventually going to solve all of the problems facing humanity; that people were good by nature; and that education would inevitably diminish humanity's barbaric tendencies. Where religion saw divine action in all unexplainable experiences, the Enlightenment saw natural phenomena that could be reasonably explained by science. Where religion argued that humans needed God in order to reach perfection, the Enlightenment believed that humanity could achieve perfectibility through its own means. Where religion saw human beings as sinners, the Enlightenment saw them as just needing proper education. Therefore, it would be through education and reason that wars would come to an end and that a utopia would emerge that would resolve all problems of work, relationships, and politics. Proper education, people believed, could minimize or remove all of the undesirable traits of humanity. Hatred, selfishness, cruelty, competition, hard-heartedness, oppression, bias, and more would all fade into history and a utopian, just, and perfect society would emerge that would never end. Humanity would have built paradise on its own terms and through its own means without help from a divine being.

A core tenant of Enlightenment thinking was the scientific method, which argued that only what could be measured and analyzed in a laboratory was real. There was no need for (or even room for) God in this worldview, and there was also no such thing as the mystical or metaphysical. If you could not measure a thing or recreate it in a lab, then it did not exist. The publication of Darwin's theory of evolution only added to the belief that there was no need for the Divine in understanding life. The Enlightenment was also deeply pragmatic; whatever worked was deemed to be "right." This thinking put a premium on anything utilitarian. It also placed supreme confidence in its own superiority: anything that could not yet be explained or understood would eventually and inevitably be understood through the relentless advancement of scientific progress.

But a funny thing happened on the way to utopia. Industrialization led to pollution, the exploitation of workers, and horrific working conditions in factories. The French Revolution led to totalitarianism and then to Napoleon. Darwinism led to theories about how best to continue the evolution of the human race, including efforts to eliminate those who were deemed genetically inferior through the eugenics program that served as a foundation of Nazi thought and contributed to the Holocaust in Europe in World War II. More recently, we have seen the Enlightenment reach its logical and destructive conclusion. In 2010, roughly thirty million Americans were taking prescription anti-depressants, which is 10 percent of the U.S. population. The twentieth century was the most violent in recorded history; communities are less safe than they were a century ago; families have broken down; and fears of impending ecological disaster are daily headlines. What happened? The goal of the Enlightenment was the triumph of individualism, global peace, and the power of human reason. What went so wrong?

First, technology is not an unconditional good. It is morally neutral, and its value depends on how it is used. Fire used to heat and cook is good, but fire used to burn down a village is bad. Chemicals that protect crops from pests and rodents are good, but those same chemicals are bad if they are then linked to groundwater contamination and incidents of cancer in children. The Enlightenment's unconditional embrace of "progress" did not take its moral neutrality into account.

The Enlightenment also failed to take into consideration the dark side of human nature. It held that education was the only tool necessary to bring about an honest, decent, and honorable society. In doing so, it underestimated the power of greed that drives people to take advantage of others; it underestimated hatred and its ability to destroy; and it underestimated the inner motives that drive people to behave in ways that are unsocial, counterproductive, and even destructive.

Another reality the Enlightenment failed to account for was the set of reactions people have to crises. Even those who have highly developed senses of integrity can change dramatically given an appropriately significant crisis. William Golding's classic, *The Lord of the Flies,* is an exploration of how quickly and easily dissension, rivalry, the development of an us-versus-them mindset and a kill-or-be-killed attitude can develop in the midst of crisis. Or, as some like to point out, human civilization is only three meals away from anarchy and unlimited barbarism.

Also, with its emphasis on only accepting what could be verified through the empirical method, the Enlightenment ultimately was incapable of addressing love, mercy, forgiveness, respect, humility, and the meaningful questions of life. When we talk of our happiest experiences, most treasured possessions, and fondest memories, they are almost all ones that have little or no rational basis for their importance. They rest on tenderness, sentimentality, and emotional value. Sometimes even the most rational biologist can tear up at the thought of a beloved childhood pet; an astrophysicist can gasp in awe at God's magnificence in a deep-field image from space; and a theoretical mathematician can be left breathless at a stirring piece of music. Do any of these pass the test of empiricism? No. Does this then mean that they are any less real? Of course not! There can be little talk of the true, the good, and the beautiful if it must be found in a test tube at a lab. For most of us, though we are unable to measure love or compassion on a scientific instrument, we do not then conclude that they do not exist. Why then do we apply such a measure in determining the legitimacy of what is holy?

Many argue that the Enlightenment ended either with the start of World War I (which used all of the advances of technology to introduce killing on an industrial scale, with tanks, aerial bombing, and poison gas), or with the dropping of the atomic bombs at the end of World War II (which showed that even the most fundamental forces of nature could be harnessed for destruction). The world is still in shock that the Enlightenment has failed. The goal of utopia has devolved into a relativized view of morality, a relativized understanding of truth, and a loss of values of any kind, and it has left in its wake a philosophical system that can identify only tolerance as being virtuous. To use a science fiction analogy, the Enlightenment ideals, exemplified by the 1980s television show *Star Trek: The Next Generation*, has given way to the moral ambiguity and suspicion of technology run amok, and the grand cosmic history of a humanity that cannot learn from its mistakes in the 2000s show *Battlestar Galactica* (a "reimagining" of the 1970s show).

In its wake, the Enlightenment, or Modernity, has been replaced by Postmodernism, which believes in no universal truths, no enduring archetypes, and no scientific or theological grounding. Its only values are individual freedom to do anything, and tolerance of others as they exercise their individual way in any manner they see fit. To sacrifice for anything or to limit the full expression and freedom of the self is the cardinal sin of postmodernism because such restraint is seen as a wasted opportunity. Postmodernism also lacks a grand narrative and an ultimate goal. The Enlightenment had its focus on using improvements in technology and education to develop a utopian paradise. Postmodernism lacks an explanation for the "why" and "how" questions of life, and also lacks an explanation for where humanity is going. Added to this unanchored worldview, the average American is bombarded with over three thousand commercial messages each per day, and these messages proclaim that true personal freedom comes from looking young, being rich, buying stuff, and focusing on sex in order to have a good life. Ironically, any ideas that would go against this particular understanding of total individual autonomy incur the full wrath of the society for being intolerant!

This ambiguity, lack of clarity, and unattainable goals (when is someone ever rich enough, young-looking enough, or sexed enough?) have left society confused and feeling empty. Without any purpose, society breaks down to its basest instincts and drifts aimlessly from one event, problem, or scandal to the next. Given this complete failure, what would a successful alternative look like? We need a radically different worldview.

A Christian Worldview

A Christian worldview is different from the other ones we have explored. It can best be described as a narrative. Christianity is not a feeling; it is not just a set of accepted propositional statements; and it is not having a sense of belonging to an institution that does good in the world. It is instead a commitment to and a relationship with Jesus that is lived out in a daily framework. The core ideas of Christianity center on the narrative that humanity was created to reflect the image of God and that each of us walks the earth for the purpose of being in an ever-deepening relationship with God, to live according to the purpose God has established for our lives, and to draw others into a relationship with God as well. However, the narrative continues and explains how, when given the choice of living our lives peacefully according to the dictates of God, or of living our lives in suffering, but as we see fit, we make the choice over and over again to live on our own terms, despite the suffering that accompanies it.

In the Garden of Eden, the point of the story is that Eve was seduced into thinking that she did not need to live as a mere creation following the rules God established. She instead became convinced that, through "knowledge of good and evil," she could instead be "like" God. Her sin was one of disobedience to God, but even more profoundly, it was one of forgetting who she was in relationship with God. This is the Original Sin of humanity. We so much want to be in control of our lives, of our surroundings, and over other people, that we forget who God is (the almighty, all-powerful, and eternal creator of the universe) and who we are (bits of dust that have been shaped by God and given the breath of life). It is out of this hubris (or arrogance, or megalomania, or whatever else you want to call it), which we all exhibit, that all of us have become estranged from God. In fact, when someone's hubris in this regard is really extreme, we say that they have a "God complex."

If this were the end of the narrative, it would only describe the dark side of humanity and leave us with the same nihilistic conclusions that postmodernism has reached. However, the story continues. Even though humanity has chosen over and over to live estranged from God, God has made repeated efforts to reconcile humanity to himself. We see such efforts in the covenant God made with Abraham, in which Abraham and his descendants were to be blessed and to bring blessings to the world, so long as they lived in the context of the relationship that

God had originally established. Of course, Abraham's descendants had a decidedly mixed track record in this regard. It seems that more often than not, they forsook the covenant and tried to follow their own ways, much to their own suffering.

However, the story still does not end there. Despite the faithlessness of the people, God continued to attempt reconciliation and sent a series of prophets over the course of hundreds of years to call each of the generations back to him and to the covenant. Sadly, in the Old Testament, we read of the harsh treatment prophets endured when their messages did not fit with the worldviews of the people hearing them. Many people today assume that the role of the prophets was to predict the future. It wasn't! Their purpose was to call an errant Israel back to its covenant with God. But when they issued their calls, they would often include a reminder of the suffering the people would incur if they did not return to God. Often, the people did not return to God, the calamities the prophets warned of would take place, and it would look like the prophets had predicted the future, when instead, their focus was really on calling people back from their mistakes and to a proper relationship with God.

Amazingly, the story of God's mercy still does not end there. In "the fullness of the time," as the Bible says (Gal. 4:4 NKJV), God chose to come to earth himself to complete the reconciliation. With the Incarnation in the person of Jesus, God no longer *told* us how to live and love, but instead *showed* us how. The ministry of Jesus served to remind us of the nature of humanity's relationship with God and about the depth of the love God has for us: "For God so loved the world that he gave his one and only Son, that whoever believes in him shall not perish but have eternal life. For God did not send his Son into the world to condemn the world, but to save the world through him." (John 3:16–17)

At the Last Supper, Jesus used the bread and wine at the table to serve as the symbols for a New Covenant, one in which reconciliation came despite our sinfulness and serial backsliding. However, to accept the offer of this new covenant, individuals are required to pledge to follow him and accept the grace that God offers to us. The New Testament describes how we are to live our lives as a result of accepting this gift.

The single greatest thing Christians can do to restore the broken relationship we have with God is to take the paradoxical step of using our free will to say to God that we are surrendering our free will to him! This may seem strange at first, but it makes sense when looked at more closely. When we use free will to serve our own ends, we often follow paths that lead to selfishness, broken relationships, and suffering. Even though most people know this to at least some degree, the behavior persists. This is original sin! If, on the other hand, we use our free will to decide that we are going to surrender it to God, then we are saying we want God to lead us; we want to live the life God desires for us; and we want to love others as God calls us to. This is the path of peace, of serenity, and of truly living the life that we were created to live.

Of course, this sounds easy, but if our worldviews do not change to support this path, we will be unable to truly follow it, even after we surrender our lives to Christ. This is why so many Christians are seen as hypocrites! They have a true and honest experience of spiritual conversion, but they do not then adjust their worldviews to reflect their newly found faith. Therefore, despite their own best efforts, they end up reverting back to old behaviors, with their associated prejudices, biases, sinfulness, and worldliness. They will continue to talk of their Christian faith and will believe they are pursuing the path of faith, but to others, they will appear unrepentant and hypocritical about what the faith teaches.

In this context, we would describe Christianity as a narrative of the ongoing relationship of God with humanity. It is a narrative that recognizes the inadequacy of human nature through our refusal to understand our place in relationship to God (original sin), the offer of reconciliation (through grace offered in the Atonement, the sacrifice of Jesus on the cross to restore humanity to God), the need to accept God's worldview (conversion), and working overtime to have God's worldview replace our own in our lives (sanctification). The goal is the establishment of God's kingdom on earth where all of humanity will live in relationship with God in the manner originally intended. This means that the "New Jerusalem" described in the New Testament book of Revelation will be what the Garden of Eden was intended to be.

Christians believe God's worldview is based on the journey of faith that each individual must decide to pursue. This is what is meant by the term "conversion." Once a person has had a conversion experience, the rest of their life is spent in the process of "sanctification," growing closer to God and manifesting God's will for them in their lives. It is a process of learning how to fully surrender to God, learning to love and forgive others, loving others unconditionally, and growing to the point where one manifests the "fruit of the Spirit" as described in chapter 5 of Galatians (the fruits are love, joy, peace, patience, kindness, goodness, faithfulness, gentleness, and self-control).

Human nature tends to be selfish, self-absorbed, short-sighted, and confused. Sanctification is the lifelong process of replacing those qualities with love for others, faith in God, and sacrifice for the building of God's kingdom on earth. Some people make the mistake of thinking that conversion must be immediately followed by perfection. In other words, once a person has a conversion experience, they should then be free from temptation, sin, and all of the other negative tendencies and emotions that plague the human condition. This could not be further from the truth! Conversion actually marks the beginning of a lifelong journey of growth. It is a journey of progress and setbacks, of sins and repentance, and struggles and triumphs. It is the process of growing (sometimes slowly, sometimes quickly), shaping, and strengthening that brings one further away from the human tendencies of selfishness and toward the goals that God has set for his children to follow. Part of the wonder and mystery of this process is that no matter how far we progress, we can never achieve perfection in this life. In writing about his own struggles with sin, Paul wrote in Romans 7:15–25a:

> I do not understand what I do. For what I want to do I do not do, but what I hate I do. And if I do what I do not want to do, I agree that the law is good. As it is, it is no longer I myself who do it, but it is sin living in me. For I know that good itself does not dwell in me, that is, in my sinful nature. For I have the desire to do what is good, but I cannot carry it out. For I do not do the good I want to do, but the evil I do not want to do—this I keep on doing. Now if I do what I do not want to do, it is no longer I who do it, but it is sin living in me that does it.

So I find this law at work: Although I want to do good, evil is right there with me. For in my inner being I delight in God's law; but I see another law at work in me, waging war against the law of my mind and making me a prisoner of the law of sin at work within me. What a wretched man I am! Who will rescue me from this body that is subject to death? Thanks be to God, who delivers me through Jesus Christ our Lord!

This is a powerful statement about the struggle with sin that even profound believers can struggle with in their lives! Sadly, it is those who try to maintain the illusion of perfection in this life who bring derision to the faith by others when they are proven to have fallen short of their professed state. An essential piece of the Christian worldview is an honest admission that each of us is a sinner. We say this not to bring condemnation on ourselves, but to be honest about the work of growth that we are all called to undertake. For Christians, sin is any thought or action that is in conflict with God's call of love, devotion, and service. Sin takes us away from God. Therefore, it is very important to understand the nature of sin, and to be mindful of how it is at work in our lives and intentional about living lives that push it further and further away from us.

Another important piece of the Christian worldview is its recognition that the struggle for holiness is not just one that takes place in the recesses of our souls and minds. We are actually part of a cosmic struggle between good and evil. Just as God seeks to draw us closer and to deepen the holiness of the relationship we were created to share, it is equally true that the devil works to draw us away from God and to destroy the holiness that is being nurtured in our souls. It is very important to remember that just as God represents all that is true, good, and beautiful, it is equally true that there is a personification of evil. This means that evil is not just a passive and unfortunate force in the universe: it has intention, deliberation, and motivation to wreak havoc on all that God desires.

Some try to argue that there really is no such thing as evil. The analogy is made of the nature of cold and heat. There is actually no such thing as cold. In chemistry, absolute zero (approximately minus 460 degrees Fahrenheit) is the temperature at which there is the complete absence of heat at the atomic level. As heat is added to or subtracted from this temperature at any point, the temperature goes up or down. So in effect, there is no such thing as cold, just the presence or absence of heat. You cannot add or take away cold, because it does not exist. You can only add or take away heat.

Using this analogy, some will argue that evil does not really exist, and that what we perceive as evil is merely the absence of the good. We can add or subtract good, but we cannot add or subtract evil, because it does not exist. The problem with this notion is that it completely misses the tug of war that takes place over the soul of every individual. It is a residual concept from the Enlightenment that tries to continue seeing people as being entirely good and capable of reaching their own perfection (if only enough good is added to the mix). A more accurate description of what happens is described by the term "spiritual warfare." This idea is based on the understanding that frailty is not just a struggle of human resolve; it is a wider struggle between the deliberate and sentient powers of good and evil, with each person being at the center of the battlefield. There are multiple participants in this battle, and it is essential for each believer to know which side they are on. By understanding the struggle in this context, one can have a better perspective of the whole situation.

People who are experienced in spiritual warfare know they are not struggling merely with emptiness but with a wily and calculating force that strikes where they tend to be the weakest. This battle is very tricky because we often fail to see how ordinary evil looks and how ordinary the holy can be. Our cultural stereotypes of the demonic tend to come either from John Milton's descriptions of demons with horns and pitchforks or from contemporary horror movies with over-the-top special effects and craziness. The truth is far more subtle and ordinary: evil can come when we give in to the temptation to badmouth another person for no other reason than the inner sense of satisfaction it brings, and holiness can come in taking joy in a household chore. C. S. Lewis talked about it this way:

> Every time you make a choice you are turning the control of part of you, the part that chooses, into something a little different from what it was before. And taking your life as a whole, with all your innumerable choices, you are slowly turning this control thing either into a heavenly creature or into a hellish one. (*Mere Christianity* 92)

A classic listing of the seven deadly sins includes lust, gluttony, greed, sloth, anger, envy, and pride. Each of these is a different manifestation of self-centeredness, misplaced priorities, or a rejection of the call of God. Actually, each one represents a whole group of sins. Each one also leads to extremes that alienate us not only from God, but also from each other and, ultimately, ourselves. Each one, if followed to its logical end, leads to death. The tragedy is that many of these sins are celebrated and glorified in our culture today.

For example, the "greed is good" speech given by the Gordon Gekko character in the 1987 movie *Wall Street* is firmly entrenched in popular culture today just as the Mae West quote "Too much of a good thing is wonderful" was anchored in the popular culture a generation ago. The problem is that when we are greedy, we focus on the object of our greed, instead of on others or God. This focus leads to jealousy and hatred for anyone who is perceived as a threat to our obtaining the object of our desire. If it is out of reach, we may take more desperate measures to get it, which always involves more alienation from others. Friends and loved ones may be reduced to little more than means to an end in our efforts to obtain the object, and more often than not, success in achieving one's desire results in a hollow victory and in the rise of greed for a goal even more difficult to obtain.

In addition to all of this, Christianity also believes that in the final analysis, we all serve a god; the only real question is which one. Is your hope and joy based on material wealth? Is it based on a particular form of satisfaction (whether physical activity, a hobby, or pure entertainment)? Is your hope and joy based on what you believe the government can do for you? Whatever you think the ultimate good is in your life is the god you serve. Each of us puts something at the center of our worldview, some idea about ourselves, or life, or our purpose. We can't help it! Nature abhors a vacuum, and something must fill that space that each of us possesses in our minds regarding spiritual reality. One of the miracles of humanity is that we actually have the opportunity to choose what that is. Many do not. They just try to move through each day like a plough horse, never paying much attention to the awe and wonder of all that God offers in this life. They go through each day with blinders on and merely react to what life throws at them. Many who succumb to the hedonistic path end up making a god in their own image in order to justify the choice of hedonism. The path is a dead end, but in a culture that idolizes the self, this path cannot be questioned, because to do so will bring the condemnation of intolerance. In the Sermon on the Mount, Jesus offers this warning: "For where your treasure is, there your heart will be also" (Matt. 6:21). Many people assume that you can use your mind to dictate what you truly treasure, which is why when many people are asked what their greatest treasures are, they will reply, "my children," "my health," or some other answer they think they are supposed to give. It is wonderful if these responses are true, but they are lies when someone claims to put their children first, but then spends very little time or energy on their children. Jesus knew this and warned that human nature is such that our heart will follow our treasure. So, instead of thinking about what we should treasure, we should pay attention to where our heart is focused, because this will reveal where the real treasure is.

If we want to truly live, we need also to understand how we currently view the world. Despite good intentions regarding living a meaningful life, our worldview may be so entrenched as to completely undermine our efforts without us even being aware. A classic example of this centers on the phenomena of people joining health clubs, only to never make use of them. Their intention is to spend the time and energy necessary to engage in a disciplined exercise regimen. They are committed to this enough to pay for the expense of a health club membership. However, if their worldview does not truly reflect this priority, then they will find it nearly impossible to follow through and to keep to the discipline of exercise. In fact, the business model of health clubs depends on this phenomenon, because they could not function profitably if most of their members actually showed up on a regular basis. True change calls us to understand our current worldview, even as we have an understanding of what we desire our worldview to be. Following the path of Jesus is not just about attending church regularly or nodding in agreement when certain things are said. It is about adopting his worldview and living our lives according to the will of God. This requires not only that we work to form a Christian worldview, but also that we work very hard at implementing it in our lives, understanding why we so often backslide, understanding God's love enough to know that we are forgiven when we ask for it, and having patience with ourselves and others as we all make the journey of sanctification.

It would be a complete waste of time to just read this chapter and move on to the next without seriously considering your current worldview. To understand what your worldview currently is, you need to be able to honestly answer some questions, which follow shortly. You will also find it very instructive to write down your answers, and compare them to what you write at the end of this book!

Warning—there is an enormous challenge in answering these questions: Our capacity for self-delusion is almost immeasurable! We tend to see ourselves in an overly positive light (unless we have a very poor self-image, in which case we will tend to see ourselves in an overly negative light). I know a

Congregationalist minister who is convinced that he is a better theologian than John Calvin; I know an unknown piano player who has talked about how he is better than Elton John; I know an aspiring author who is convinced that his self-published book is better than anything ever written by Ernest Hemingway; I know an Anglican priest in a small parish who is convinced that he has a much more compelling vision for church than Bill Hybels does, and I know that I have my own delusions about what will become of this book. It is very hard to be honest with oneself! In addressing the questions that follow, you need to be careful not to answer them as you would like the answers to be or feel the answers should be ("since I am a Christian, I should say God is the most important thing in my life, even though, in reality, my car is"). You also want to be sure you do not overstate your virtues and understate your sins (or vice versa).

Though it may seem like a commonsense warning, it is easier said than done. Personality tests (like Myers-Briggs, DISC, and the Enneagram) can do much to help someone understand their traits, habits, and dispositions, but the biggest problem they have is in getting test-takers to be honest about themselves. In these tests, each issue is asked in a variety of different ways with the hopes that honest answers will tend to prevail (which is why some tests have over 140 questions). For this particular book, we do not have a diagnostic instrument like a personality test for you to take—instead, spend time in prayerful and honest reflection on each question and ask people who are very close to you what they think of the answers you come up with. See where God leads you!

The questions to ponder are as follows:

- If you had to sum up your life in a single sentence, what would it be?
- What has your allocation of time and energy shown is the most important thing in your life?
- What would you like to have as your life's purpose?
- Is there a single verse or passage of the Bible that most clearly defines or articulates your faith?
- What spiritual gifts do you have?
- Can you name specifically why you love Jesus?
- What are you most committed to?
- Can you name who needs your love the most?
- What are the most significant daily routines you have?
- Is there anyone you actively pray for on a daily basis? Who and why?
- What do you do for fun?
- What is the most important thing you do for your family?
- What do you do to serve your church?
- What do you do to serve others in your community?
- What is the biggest sacrifice you are making in your life right now?
- What is your greatest weakness? What are you doing about it right now?
- What are your greatest goals in life?

These questions are a great starting point for the process the rest of this book will lead you through. In the next chapter, we will wrestle more with this process of discernment and then get to the core tasks of developing a personal Rule for Life.

3

The Discernment
of Spirits

"The unexamined life is not worth living."

—Socrates, in Plato's *The Apology of Socrates*

I once served on the board of directors for a nonprofit agency in my community. The members of the board came from a variety of walks of life and had different goals in serving the agency. "Shelly" was a relatively young member of the board and was perhaps one of its most vocal members.

At one meeting, we got into a discussion of the fruit of the Spirit as described in Galatians 5:22–23 (again, those are love, joy, peace, patience, kindness, goodness, faithfulness, gentleness, and self-control). As part of an interesting exercise, someone asked if we could rate our personal progress in each of the nine areas. Shelly jumped in, and as she read the list, she stated that she was doing well in most of the areas, with perhaps the exception of patience. She saw herself as loving, joyful, kind, gentle, and everything else on the list. But, in perhaps an effort to ensure she remained humble, she did express the need to learn how to be more patient.

No one said a word, but most of the people were thinking the same thing. Shelly was an argumentative, confrontational, and bitter person who was angry at a lack of personal professional success and tended to react with open hostility when she did not get her way. In fact, within a year, she was asked by the board chair to step down because of her inability to work well with others.

How does this happen? How did she see herself in such a profoundly different light than everyone else did? If this were the only case of it I ever encountered, then she could easily be dismissed as being delusional; but truth be told, Shelly's behavior is not uncommon at all. There is an old saying that goes, "We do not see the world as it is; we see it as we are." I think that there should be the corollary, "We do not see ourselves as we are; we see ourselves as we want to be." If we decide that our problems, struggles, and failures are actually the fault of someone else, we will hold a wildly optimistic view of ourselves and just conclude that we are the victims of someone else's incompetence or caprice. Of course, this is not the real world! It is a classic situation in which everyone who drives slower than us on the highway is a moron and everyone who drives faster than us is an idiot. We hold an idealized view of ourselves if we choose not to see that we are actually much messier in how we live our lives than we like to think we are.

The human capacity for self-deception is virtually unlimited. We can talk ourselves out of or into anything! We can overstate or dismiss any experience or event to make us into the people we want to be in our minds. If I do not get along with the other board members, I can blame them for their ignorance, lack of vision, poor leadership, or their spite for me. The mere fact that everyone sees me as argumentative and impossible to work with doesn't have to enter into my conscious thought process at all!

Where do our self-images come from? We know that God gives each of us a set of specific spiritual gifts. Added to this are the imprints left by our family of origin (values, culture, and family sins). These are things we have limited control over, and they, in essence, mark our starting point. We are then affected by our society, friends, career choices, and by how we react to what happens to us. We are indeed haunted by our mistakes, fears, failures, bad experiences, broken hearts, and family of origin issues. We can also be filled with hopes, anxieties, or even the mood of any given day. We try to listen for the voice of God but find it hard to distinguish it from the voice of the devil, or even from our own voice. Rather than be honest, we tend to see ourselves in too positive a light by seeing ourselves as we want to be, rather than as we are, or we see ourselves in too negative a light and conclude the worst.

This situation is fiendishly complex. Can it be dealt with and understood? Absolutely! I am a graduate of a Jesuit high school. My school constantly reminded its students of Socrates' declaration that "The unexamined life is not worth living" (Plato 38A). Since my teenage years, I have been reflecting on my life as I live it and trying to learn what I can from my own experiences and from the experiences of those around me. To make progress in my spiritual pilgrimage, I have had to take long and hard looks at bad patterns of behavior, faulty understandings about life, a selfish streak, a perfectionist streak, a willingness to put goals before people, and most recently, a need to live focused on the positive instead of the negative. I constantly reflect on how I live my life—how I serve Christ and his church, how I bear witness to the Good News, and whom I choose to serve all matter, and I must be intentional about them. Life should not be lived by just reacting to what happens around us. Life should be lived on purpose and with purpose, as Rick Warren has so eloquently argued!

It is for all of these reasons that an honest appraisal about the issues explored in this book should include a reflection on what St. Ignatius of Loyola called the "discernment of spirits" (388). This chapter explains how to evaluate the spiritual significance of various thoughts, feelings, and actions and how they relate to spiritual well-being.

Our Context

Our culture has fallen into a trap of pseudo-self-reflection. People try to stay positive, wish for good things to happen, or try to remind themselves that they are already the best they can be. These efforts are vapid, self-indulgent, and self-centered. There is a popular yoga studio near where I live where the instructors spend the entire lesson telling the participants how wonderful they are and reminding them of how spiritually fulfilling it really is to stretch out and pamper themselves. They are told that if they feel good about themselves, they are on the path to wisdom. With little other experience to compare this to, it is not surprising that few can discern whether this is a shallow narcissism or a genuine spirituality.

But it fits with our culture's core values of sex, youth, wealth, fame, and diversity. The belief is that if you look younger, have more sex, make more money, become more famous, and accept anything that anyone else does—then you will be happier. This prescription isn't working. Despite being richer than any society ever has been, we are desperately sad today. A significant research study conducted by the Centers for Disease Control and Prevention (the National Health and Nutrition Examination of 2005–2008), found that by 2008, more than 11 percent of Americans were on prescription antidepressants or antianxiety medications. More than 60 percent of them have been on medication for at least two years, and 14 percent have been on medication for more than ten years. The study also showed that antidepressants are the third most common prescription drug taken in the U.S. and the most frequently used medication by people between the ages of 18 and 44.

The American Journal of Psychiatry, in a similar study, found that depression rates for American adults more than doubled in a single recent decade, from 3.33 percent in 1991 to 7.06 percent in 2002. The rate of diagnosing and prescribing medication for such conditions has accelerated since then.

How is it that our culture has more money, leisure time, and entertainment opportunities than any other culture in the history of the world, yet we are desperately alone, afraid, and depressed? The problem is that human beings were never meant to focus on themselves. We have turned happiness into a goal instead of a side benefit. Our lives are not meant to be happy; they are meant to be meaningful. If we seek to lead happy lives, we will invariably focus on shallow pursuits and never attain true happiness. If we lead meaningful lives, then we will truly be happy! True reflection lies in a sober assessment and understanding of where we are in life. It is an honest admission of our failures, a healthy identification of where our struggles are, a realistic understanding of the good going on in our lives, and a Christ-centered effort to plot our position on the map of life and to move in the direction God calls us. We don't do this to judge or condemn ourselves. To do that would completely miss the point of the exercise. To see ourselves for who we really are can be painful, but the good news is that God loves us, offers forgiveness, and calls us to a better life! Knowing where we have been and where we are makes it easier to see where God is calling us to go.

Equally important, this exercise is not done to improve self-awareness or to celebrate all we are. We are *not* the center of attention, and we are not the main actor on the stage—God is. So our main task is to identify what God is doing and find what part of it God wants us to do. When we live with God at the center of life, we can fulfill the role we were created to fulfill, and we can know happiness. When we try to be in control ourselves, we are trying to fulfill God's role, and this strategy is guaranteed to end poorly.

When you think about it, this understanding makes our lives even more meaningful because it means that God has called each of us to a sacred task, and we take our faith seriously enough to do the work necessary to obey the call, which is one of healing, growth, service, and sacrifice.

This pilgrimage should not be taken alone. Human nature is such that we too quickly become a small boat tossed upon a stormy sea of a tumultuous mind. We *must* make the journey with other people who can serve as our anchor, our compass, and the wind for our sails when necessary. For Christians, this is why we must be in a church. The messy, difficult, and awkward journey goes much better when we have others who are on the same journey and who can share struggles, questions, celebrations, and victories with us. More on that later.

So, how do we hear God's voice in our lives?

Real Spiritual Growth

In one of her comedy acts, Lily Tomlin asked, "Why is it when we talk to God we're said to be praying—but when God talks to us, we're said to be schizophrenic?" We are comfortable with the idea of talking to God, but how do we listen? God speaks to different people in different ways. A big part of the challenge is learning how to hear God's voice in your unique life.

We get a phenomenal example of how God speaks in 1 Kings 19. After what seemed like a wildly successful confrontation with pagan prophets in his fight to preserve the true faith of Israel, Elijah is forced to flee for his life because the Israelite queen favored the pagan gods over the Lord of Israel. He eventually makes his way to Mt. Sinai and is in total despair over what is to become of him. In this beautiful moment, we see God arrive to speak to him. We read that Elijah heard a loud wind and looked for God's voice in the wind, but it wasn't there. He next experienced an earthquake and looked for the voice of God in the earthquake, but it wasn't there. Next, there was a great fire, but God's voice wasn't in the fire, either. Finally, we are told that Elijah heard a "still, small voice," and it was in this gentle whisper that he heard God speak to him.

I think this story is poignant because we all too often call out to God in desperation and expect a great fire or an earthquake to accompany God speaking. But more often than not, we hear the still, small voice, so it is essential that we be able to hear it. But here's the catch: When we listen for God's voice, we usually do not hear one voice; we hear at least three. Like the cartoon image of an angel standing on one shoulder and the devil standing on the other, we try to hear God and end up in a debate between ourselves, God, and the devil.

God's voice will speak his will; our voice tells us what we think we want to hear; and the devil's voice will tempt us to follow any appealing path that will draw us away from God. How can you make progress if you can't distinguish between these three voices? Each one has a different goal. Each one is desperate to get you to follow it. Each one knows exactly which buttons to push (but of the three, only God chooses not to push them). Sometimes, this can be like listening to a radio where all of the stations are playing simultaneously. With the conglomeration of songs, talk, and commercials all playing at once, how can anything meaningful be distinguished?

It is essential to learn the difference. For some people, the voices sound different from each other. For others, the voices are in a different tone. And for still others, the voices may be heard coming from different directions. For me, God is heard in my heart, my own voice is heard in my gut, and the devil's voice is heard from behind me. So, before embarking on discovering God's call for our life and developing our Rule for Life, we must first learn to distinguish God's voice in the midst of the noise. There are a number of ways to do this. I have found one developed by St. Ignatius of Loyola to be particularly helpful.

Ignatius of Loyola

To be better able to distinguish between the voices, St. Ignatius of Loyola (1491–1556) offers a guide. Ignatius was born into a wealthy family from Northern Spain in 1491. Growing up as a semi-aristocrat, he fantasized of earlier times of chivalry and glorious battles. He entered the army hoping to find glory, but in May 1521, he was wounded in a battle against the French at Pamplona. During his fairly lengthy convalescence, he turned to reading to help pass the time. He found that he enjoyed reading books on chivalry and battle, but the feelings of enjoyment and satisfaction quickly passed after putting the books down. After running out of these types of books, he came across a book on the lives of different saints. Upon reading this, he was deeply touched and discovered that a feeling of joy stayed with him long after he had put the book down. This was the beginning of his discovery of the process of discernment and of the power of the different voices that try to influence us.

He describes this discovery in his autobiography, referring to himself in the third person:

> When he was thinking of those things of the world he took much delight in them, but afterwards, when he was tired and put them aside, he found himself dry and dissatisfied. But when he thought of going to Jerusalem barefoot, and of eating nothing but plain vegetables and of practicing all the other rigors that he saw in the saints, not only was he consoled when he had these thoughts, but even after putting them aside he remained satisfied and joyful. (71)

This experience led to his conversion to a devout Christian life. After a number of years of spiritual growth, Ignatius and a group of companions formed the Society of Jesus (more commonly known today as the Jesuits) and were commissioned to become teachers. By the time he died in 1556, the Jesuits had a thousand members and had started thirty-three colleges (and he had approved six more). Today, Jesuit schools and universities are known all over the world. In the United States, Fordham University, Loyola University, Georgetown University, Boston College, and Gonzaga University are just some of the Jesuit schools.

Another of his great accomplishments was to develop a method for the discernment of spirits (distinguishing between the voices and their actions), and another was the development of a set of spiritual exercises to be used in the context of a thirty-day retreat that leads the retreatant through an intense journey of growth. Together, these all define a distinct system of Ignatian spirituality.

The Ignatian path is one that leads to a disciplined process of reflection on the actions and experiences of our lives. Its goal is to help us find a spiritual maturity that not only endures in this life, but also makes a difference in the lives and faith of others. Though much time is spent reflecting on our mistakes and struggles, the goal is to grow to a place of holiness and truth, which includes a life lived with few regrets. In fact, in his life, Ignatius only feared having one regret. In reflecting on his own life, he wrote,

> Another time, while he was going by sea from Valencia to Italy in a violent storm, the rudder of the ship was

broken, and the situation reached such a pass that in his judgment and that of many others who sailed on the ship, they could not by natural means escape death. At this time, examining himself carefully and preparing to die, he could not feel afraid for his sins or of being condemned, but he did feel embarrassment and sorrow, as he believed he had not used well the gifts and graces which God our Lord had granted him. (81–82)

Ignatian Spirituality

For St. Ignatius, the discernment of spirits came through a process called the Examination of Conscience, or the Examen, for short. The goal of the Examen is to gain insight into why things are as they are so that we can move toward the way things are meant to be. The discipline is actually quite simple. It is best summed up as experience followed by reflection on that experience. In the Examen, we seek to see our day as Jesus sees it: free from deception, pain, ego, and confusion. Over time, we develop the ability to leave the chaos of the Fall behind and come to see everything in life through the eyes of Jesus. The Examen is made up of five steps. You prepare by finding a place where you can have twenty minutes or more of quiet, uninterrupted prayer time and begin with a time of transition during which you think about the magnitude of God's love for you and about how much God is a part of your process of growth. You then proceed to the five specific steps, outlined by Timothy Gallagher as follows:

1. A time to note the gifts that God has given you today. Where have the consolations been found, and how did you react to them? The goal of this step is to develop

a sensitivity to the many ways in which God speaks to us.

2. A time of petition to ask God for insight, help, and clarity as you engage in this reflection.

3. A detailed review of the day. Good things and bad things should both be noted. Reflect on the decisions that were made, the choices that were made, and the interactions that were had with other people. Then reflect on how they went, how they made you feel, and if they were unsatisfactory, how you would have liked to have dealt with them.

4. A time to seek forgiveness. When desolations are noted, ask for forgiveness. When you make note of burdens that are weighing you down, ask God to lift them from your shoulders. If you need to ask the forgiveness of others, resolve to seek it within twenty-four hours.

5. A time for renewal. After you have noted the consolations God has sent to you, reflected on the struggles that you experienced, and sought forgiveness, the time has come to look to the upcoming day and to ask God for help in specific areas of need. In doing this, and in developing a mindfulness of where you are trying to grow, this is where spiritual growth comes! (25–28)

As you wrap up this process of reflection, it is important to be thankful, to contemplate the power of God's forgiveness, and to remember how much God wants to be a part of the process of growth. God's desire is to lead us into growth, not to judge us for failure to grow! The Examen is always future-focused, not past-focused. We do not use the past to endlessly relive past successes or to dwell on past failures; we use it as a way to help us see where we are and to point to the future.

The Examen is an important spiritual discipline because it puts everything else we do in context. It is a daily reality check that helps ensure we are following the Christian path that Jesus has laid out for us and have not gone off on some strange tangent that leads to nowhere good. Ideally, it should be done for at least twenty minutes at a time and at least once a day. Twice is better. By doing this exercise over time, we gain an understanding of how God speaks life and truth, and of how our own minds and the voice of the devil try to draw us away. It is through seeing how following each voice affects us that we learn to distinguish God's voice more clearly.

This is a significant exercise, and like physical exercise, it is a very hard discipline in the beginning. But with practice and perseverance, it becomes a wonderfully beneficial part of our day. Over time, it becomes something that is very hard to do without; and with experience, it becomes easier to distinguish between the three (or perhaps more) voices in our heads.

One of the most significant challenges of the Examen comes because we bring our own expectations of how we believe God should act in particular situations and in our lives. When God's actions differ from our expectations, we not only despair what appears to be seemingly unanswered prayer, but we miss the glorious actions of God in our lives! It is a fundamental characteristic of human nature that we want to be in control of our lives. This is a direct result of the Fall and of the damaged relationship that humanity has with God. We are not content to be the creature and to allow God to be the creator. We are not content to be the clay and to allow God to be the potter. We want to call the shots. We want events in life to unfold in a certain way, and sometimes even though the events do eventually happen, that fact gets lost in our frustration that they didn't happen just as we wanted them to. It is wrong to demand certain outcomes of God. It is equally wrong to think that if we surrender the outcome to God's control, we can still make demands on the journey taken to get to those goals!

For Ignatius, the key to the Examen is complete trust in the ever-present love of God. God's love flows through his actions in our life each day. It is manifested in the forgiveness that God freely offers when we ask, and we respond when we seek to draw closer to God through how we plan to approach the upcoming day. If our Examen is not grounded first in the reality of God's love for us, then we not only miss the point, we also risk trying to do the work out of fear or some other impure motive. It must also be grounded in a mature understanding of Christian for-giveness, which is not just about letting go of sin or failure, but is also about becoming more Christlike. God does offer complete restoration of relationship when we seek it, but his forgiveness doesn't end there. It is offered as a means by which we can then learn from mistakes and become more Christlike. It is offered to help us grow into the people God has created us to be. This is a powerful and holy pilgrimage! If we accept forgiveness without the understanding that it serves a holy purpose, then it has no real meaning.

John 3:16 is one of the best-known passages of Scripture: "For God so loved the world that he gave his one and only Son, that whoever believes in him shall not perish but have eternal life." This is used as a key argument for the need for faith in

Christ. However, what often gets overlooked is the next verse! In verse 17, we read, "For God did not send his Son into the world to condemn the world, but to save the world through him." These two verses together are so significant! The mission of Jesus is to save the world, not because we are good, but because of God's love for us: a love we have not earned and a love that we do not deserve. But it is there! This is a unique and profound aspect of Christianity, because Christianity is the only major world religion where the emphasis is on forgiveness and on the grace of God. Hinduism and Buddhism follow the law of karma, and in karma, you cannot find forgiveness. The best you can hope for is to accumulate enough good karma to offset the bad karma you have earned through your mistakes. Though no longer emphasized, Judaism was built on the notion of proportional justice, epitomized in the idea of "an eye for an eye, and a tooth for a tooth" (see Exod. 21:24, Matt. 5:38 KJV). In Islam, there is swift judgment for any infractions of Sharia law. Christian grace focuses on forgiveness, help from God in growing, and forgiveness for mistakes along the pilgrimage of growth with God, who never gives up. As Simone Weil once wrote, "God waits like a beggar who stands motionless and silent before someone who will perhaps give him a piece of bread. Time is that waiting. Time is God's waiting as a beggar for our love" (141). For Christians, the goal is a relationship with Christ that is grounded in love, and with that relationship comes growth and a process of maturation that leads us to the purpose of our creation. Or, as Ignatius himself wrote with regard to his spiritual exercises: "The one thing we desire, the one thing we choose is what is more likely to achieve the purpose of our creating" (Corbishley 22).

Consolation and Desolation

As described above, an important aspect of the discernment of spirits is understanding the roles that Consolation and Desolation play in our pilgrimage. For Ignatius, these are where we see the work of God taking place in our daily lives. Both are used by God as well as by the devil to pull us closer or to drive us away from God.

A Consolation is an experience of peace, serendipity, or joy. There are no limits to the ways one can happen. It can be a kind word from someone, the quiet joy of a job well done, a moment of inspiration, a reassurance that all will be well, a warm day in winter, a cool breeze in summer, a tender touch, a look of love, loving attention from a pet, the laughter of a child, a particularly funny moment, the comfort of friends, or the song of a bird. One of the blessings of life is that the moments of Consolation are endless!

Consolations, however, are not mountaintop experiences. They are not emotional or spiritual highs. Those moments are exceptions to the normal. They are wonderful gifts and blessings from God, but they are not meant for daily support. This distinction is important because some people become addicted to the adrenaline of mountaintop experiences and conclude that those are the only true encounters with God that we experience in life. Sadly, because these tend to be few and far between, people hunting for them can grow despondent over their infrequency and actually lose faith because of it. Consolations, on the other hand, do happen daily. We just need to be cognizant of them and celebrate them. Too often, we downplay or dismiss them as coincidences, we are too distracted by our troubles to see them, or we somehow give ourselves credit for them. When we do any of these things, we miss them! In learning the discernment of spirits, we gain a greater awareness of consolations and develop an appreciation for the role they play in daily life.

Desolations can be one of two things. They can be a test from God or a temptation from the devil. When they are a test from God, they are a time when we are left to our own strength to test our reliance on God. In these moments of emptiness, we learn how strong our trust in God is, and we are reminded of how little control we really have in life. It is a time to cultivate humility, patience, and perseverance. It is also an important reminder that we cannot make the pilgrimage through this life on our own. We must remain centered on God in the good times as well as in the bad.

The other kind of desolations are ones the devil uses to tempt us away from God. These are times when we feel like we may have found a shortcut through a difficult issue, we have used others to accomplish a selfish goal, or we have such a strong sense of ourselves that we forget our reliance on God. All of these may offer momentary joy, but like the crash after a sugar high, they are followed by an unpleasant emptiness.

Desolations can be tricky because the devil will do his best to disguise them. Sometimes, we feel desolation not because something bad or painful has happened, but because we didn't get things to happen just the way we wanted them to. A child in a store may convince you to make one impulsive purchase, and perhaps even a second one, but if they fail at the third, then they leave feeling as if they have failed. They do not celebrate the victories, but rather focus on the one defeat and feel unloved.

Ignatius experienced the very same thing! He writes of an experience when God gave him the answer he wanted (related to whether his new religious order should live in poverty) but didn't do it in the manner he wanted, and this gap left him with a feeling of desolation. Upon reflection in the Examen, he realized that God had done exactly what he had hoped God would, but he needed to let God do it in God's way, not his own. This was a powerful lesson and is not one we easily learn on our own without the Examen!

The Role of Community

I remember taking a class on Ascetical Theology a number of years ago. When we were discussing the spiritual exercises, an Episcopal seminarian was overwhelmed with the intensity of what the retreatant was to experience, and he drew the conclusion that Ignatius must have been like a drill sergeant who barked orders at his retreatants so they could accomplish all he intended for them to. He thought that Ignatius meant for the exercises to break the person down so that he could build him or her back up again. This couldn't be further from the truth! Though the content of the Ignatian disciplines is intense, it is not meant to be hard or painful for those who practice it! In fact, in writing about how to conduct his four-week set of spiritual exercises, Ignatius offers this guidance to those who will lead them:

> If the retreat-giver sees that the retreatant is undergoing distress and temptation, he must not be harsh or severe but kind and considerate, encouraging and strengthening him for what is ahead, exposing the tricks of the enemy of mankind, reassuring him and doing all he can to put him in a suitable frame of mind for the comfort in store. (14, note 7)

This is a great example of why community is so important to Christianity and how people need to be around others, not only to help them on their pilgrimages, but to be helped as well. There are many ways in which this reality check can happen, from participation in congregational life, in small groups, and in support groups, to being accountable to a clergy person, having a prayer partner, having a spiritual director, or having a confessor. The specific method or methods used are not as important as the discipline of living in community with other Christians.

Jesus never intended for us to make the journey alone—that is why he gave us the church. In North America and Europe, where individualism reigns, many people make the mistake of thinking they can "do it alone." This is an example of local culture trying to supersede theological truth. The theological truth is that God has called us together in community and it is in community that we best hear God's voice and that we best work out our salvation, "with fear and trembling" (Phil. 2:12).

In community, we can have a trusted friend tell us that our discernment may be drifting just a bit toward the delusional. We can get a reality check, and we can be there to help others as they make their pilgrimages of growth and Christian development. Community is also where we learn to love people who annoy us, to be patient with people who aggravate us, and to help people we would rather ignore. And community allows others who are bothered by *our* idiosyncrasies and shortcomings to learn to do the same!

Perhaps the hardest part of learning to discern spirits is that it takes time. We need to learn how to be quiet so we can listen. Imagine having a friend who did 100 percent of the talking in your relationship. It wouldn't be much of a friendship. Yet we blithely call ourselves friends of God and make no effort at all at listening to anything God has to say. We must also be able to discern which voice we are hearing. When God is calling us to a hard path, we may be very tempted to follow our own voice and convince ourselves that it is God's; or we may go down the path to the dark side by listening to the temptations of the devil and trying to convince ourselves that this is the voice of God (something that seems to happen disproportionately to televangelists, but that is a topic for another book).

The more active and noisy your life is, the harder this will be to learn. Our culture is designed to keep us from engaging in any meaningful reflection! Everything is noise and distraction. We hear noise from the moment we wake up in the morning until it is time for bed. We then go to bed and start it all over the next day. We have become a society of consumers, and we consume information and entertainment nonstop. A very common problem among the young (and many of the not-so-young) is the inability to go more than five minutes without checking their phone for calls, texts, or social media posts.

All of this noise conspires against us, and we need to learn how to turn it all off. Only then can we contemplate what consolations God has given us during the previous day and recognize the moments of desolation. Then we can listen for the voice of God and distinguish it from the other voices so that we can understand God's will for a particular situation and receive the encouragement to actually follow in obedience.

This is all so very important! To develop a Rule for Life, we need to be people who grow. In order to grow, we need to implement and use spiritual disciplines. To engage the disciplines in a meaningful manner, we need to be honest about where we are in life and where we are really going. The process of discernment of spirits and the ability to distinguish between consolations and desolations and to understand the role that each plays in our formation as mature Christians is of the utmost importance. Of all the spiritual disciplines that you can engage in, this is the first one to develop! If you start developing the habit of using this discipline now, it will be of enormous help as you work your way through the rest of this book.

Questions for Reflection

1. Can you distinguish between the voice of God, the voice of the devil, and your own voice? If not, why? If so, how?

2. Spend twenty minutes in the process of Examen as described in this chapter. When done, describe how you felt during the experience—what stood out and what do you feel called to do as a response to the experience?

3. We are a culture of individualists, but we are called to be together as the church. How do you respond when you feel the church does not serve you well? What response does Jesus call for?

4. What are three specific steps you can take in order to incorporate the Examen into your daily life?

A Rule for Life

"Let nothing, therefore, be put before the Work of God."

—St. Benedict of Nursia, *The Rule of Saint Benedict*

Faith is not a "nice idea" or just something to be debated. In fact, theological debates are often used as the means to avoid the real work of living by the principles articulated in Scripture. There is an old joke told in seminaries that if a theologian is given the choice of going to heaven or attending a lecture about heaven, he or she would choose the lecture. After all, if you are given the choice of arguing over how many angels can dance on the head of a pin, or making changes to your life to better fit the call of God, the argument is much easier to have than the change is to make! When the Apostle Paul arrived in Athens, "All the Athenians and the foreigners who lived there spent their time doing nothing but talking about and listening to the latest ideas" (Acts 17:21). Paul's task was to show them that faith was a lifestyle, not a philosophical construct; that it is about a life to be lived, not an argument to be won. Having the correct belief is of tremendous importance, but it has to be lived, not just believed.

The true goal of the Christian life is to manifest our love for God and love for our neighbor in every action of every day of our lives. To do this, we need a structure within which to live daily life. The growing pressures of conformity to a secular and hedonistic culture make it very important that we name and live the life that we say we intend to. Though this may seem odd to some at first, a great model to consider is the one St. Benedict developed for monasteries in the early sixth century. No, really! When asked to establish communities for monks, Benedict wrote a Regula, or Rule, to guide and govern daily life in the monastic community. The Rule was created to help people develop a disciplined spiritual life in the midst of a decadent and depraved society at the end of the Roman Empire. This model has much to offer today, but it first helps to understand how it arose and what its core principles are.

Context

In the years and decades after the resurrection of Jesus, the church spread rapidly throughout the Roman Empire. (The early stages of this growth are recorded in the biblical book of Acts.) The Roman Empire was a smorgasbord of ethnic, cultural, religious, and social groups. Each had differing values, priorities, and worldviews. The overarching principle of the empire was that all of these differences were to be tolerated so that public order could be maintained. Local customs were allowed to continue; the people could pray to different gods and live by different standards. However, everyone living in the empire had to refrain from politically subversive activity, pay their taxes, and obey Roman law. Other than that, the empire was only interested in maintaining order, so one group showing intolerance toward another was seen as completely unacceptable, as it was absolutely essential that everyone get along. Also, even though the people could worship any god or goddess, they also had to accept the Roman Emperor as a divine being and pray to him. For most people, this was not a problem. Since they practiced pagan religions, they were accustomed to having many gods and goddesses in their religious life, so adding one more would not be much of a threat to their faith. In their daily and weekly religious rituals, they made offerings to and on behalf of the emperor.

This system posed two significant problems for Christians. The first was that the moral norms of the empire were incredibly permissive and lax. Almost any kind of behavior was deemed acceptable, so long as it didn't threaten public order. Christians knew that if they wanted to maintain their moral and theological values, they had to live in a manner that was significantly countercultural. This also meant that they had to try and raise their children with values and ideals that were far different from those of their friends. The second problem was that though most people freely accepted adding the emperor as one more god to their personal pantheon of deities, Christians, who believed that there could be only one God, could not do so. The empire saw this refusal as a political challenge more than as a theological one, and the tension played a significant role in early persecutions of the church. During the church's first three hundred years, there were frequent outbreaks of persecution, ranging from vandalism of property to job losses, imprisonment, and even execution. Many Christians practiced their faith in secret, while others did so openly knowing the risks. This generally meant that churches were made up of people who were deeply committed and highly motivated. The support and commitment that people in the community showed to one another was very intense and their relationship with God guided all decision-making. People in the church also lived and practiced the faith knowing that at any time, their lives could be destroyed. There were certainly no fair-weather Christians in the early church! Those who were there were literally willing to die for their faith.

Because of the tensions and struggles this created between church and culture, some Christians concluded that the best way to deal with the problem was to abandon the pagan and hedonistic society altogether. The decadence of Roman society was seen as having a corrosive effect on Christian formation, so from the third century on, many fled to the deserts of Egypt, where they struggled to learn the will of God on their own. Through imitating the temptation of Jesus in the desert, they fasted, did battle with the devil, and sought to draw closer to God. Some became influential and important writers about the faith, and they are known as the "Desert Fathers." St. Anthony the Great (251–356), St. Athanasius (296–373), St. John Cassian (360–435), and St. John Chrysostom (347–407) are perhaps the best known of this group. Through contemplation, isolation, and extreme asceticism, they developed an intense form of Christian living.

After AD 313, with Emperor Constantine's conversion to the Christian faith, it became legal to practice Christianity openly within the empire. This brought significant changes. Admission into the church became easy, the intensity of church life waned, and the church slowly came to look more and more like the empire itself. Within a generation or two, the culture was changing the church more than the church was changing the culture. It was now respectable, instead of countercultural, to be Christian. By AD 380, Emperor Theodosius I decreed that Christianity was to be the only legal religion. All other religions were outlawed. People were now Christian by imperial decree rather than by a profession of faith. People were now baptized because it was the social norm rather than because they had experienced a profound conversion to the faith. There was no longer a special sense of community, because everyone belonged to the church by default. Evangelism was no longer needed, and instead of working to convert one's neighbors, the only people in need of conversion were those who lived outside of the boundaries of the empire. People no longer needed to share their faith with anyone, and soon forgot how to do so. This all led to a watered down and institutionally driven church. Passion for Jesus was replaced by a sense of loyalty to the institution, and the organizational structure of the church came to resemble that of the government—which is why the church was not based in Jerusalem; the Western church was based in the Western imperial capital of Rome and the Eastern church was based in the Eastern imperial capital of Constantinople. The corrupting influence of society on the church led many devout Christians to fear that it was becoming too difficult to truly hold to the high standards set forth by Jesus. It was in this context that the phenomenon of hermits living in the Egyptian desert evolved into more organized monastic communities.

St. Benedict of Nursia

It was into this era of growth and tension that Benedict of Nursia was born. St. Benedict (AD 480–547) is considered the "father of Western monasticism." (St. Basil is seen as the father of Eastern monasticism.) Benedict was the son of a wealthy nobleman and lived a life of comfort and luxury. Despite this, he developed an inner doubt that wealth could lead to a meaningful life. Eventually, he left home and began searching for a different answer. As the story goes, after meeting a monk, he was so moved by the experience that he decided to become a hermit and spent most of the next three years in solitary contemplation. However, he did have contact with other monks, and when one group lost its leader, his reputation was such that they pressured him to become their leader. After initial resistance, he agreed to serve as abbot. Sadly, the relationship did not work out well.

There is a story that tells of them trying to poison him in order to get rid of him. They poisoned his drink, but in offering a blessing over it, the cup shattered. They then tried to poison his bread, but as he offered a blessing over it, a raven swooped into the room and took it. Fortunately, he left and returned to his hermit cave before they could try another attempt. All this only added to his reputation for piety and holiness. Eventually, he was asked again to develop monastic communities, so he oversaw the building of twelve monasteries with twelve monks in each. He also built a thirteenth monastery, which he led himself. Benedict spent the rest of his life perfecting his model for monasticism and sought to achieve a balance of prayer, work, and devotional consistency. He died at his monastery at Monte Cassino (about eighty miles southeast of Rome) in 547. Benedictine monasteries still exist all over the world, and Benedictine spirituality is deeply ingrained in many diverse places throughout Christendom.

Central to life in the monasteries was the official set of rules that Benedict developed to govern them. It is called, in Latin, a Regula, or in English, a Rule. The Latin term literally means "a straight stick." As a stick, it serves as the "ruler" against which everything in monastic life is to be measured against. The ideal was to have a balance of prayer, study, and work. The monastic life was not meant to physically punish the monks, but it was also not meant to free them from hard work. Benedict also saw that the daily routine of monastic life needed to revolve around times of community prayer. The Benedictine motto, "ora et labora" means "pray and work." Each is of great importance, and each is to be done in that order. It is out of prayer and devotion to God that work and service to others flow. It cannot exist the other way around—we cannot effectively use service to others as our entry into a deeper relationship with God. This leads to the misguided notion that our works can earn us a place in heaven, which the Protestant reformer Martin Luther argued against in the sixteenth century. It must be out of our relationship with God that we then serve others. In other words, there must be a balance of both prayer and work, but the work must come as a result of the prayer. The love for God developed in prayer is so deep that it compels us to seek ways to serve his people.

Benedict's Rule has seventy-three short chapters and is the only book he ever wrote. Though he wrote it to serve as little more than an introduction to monastic life, it is still the most widely used Rule in the world today. More than half of the chapters focus on how to be humble and obedient, as well as how to deal with others who are not. In Benedictine spirituality, the goal is for the practitioner to engage in a process of deepening obedience to God and the gradual strengthening of a union with God. The role of the Rule is to create the structure within which the individual renounces his or her own free will and engages in the hard work of learning obedience. This structure is very important. Just as architects use a compass to draw a curved line that defines the boundaries of a circle, the Rule encircles the life of the monk. It serves to define his values, his priorities, and his limits. It leaves no doubt as to where the boundaries are and to where the forces and activities that would be harmful to spiritual development are to be found. The rule brings definition and clarity to life so that life is lived intentionally and deliberately, not accidentally. This may appear rather simple and perhaps even obvious, but most people never go through a process of defining their lives. They instead merely react to events around them and are unknowingly shaped by those events. The world molds them into its image more than they mold the world into God's image. Hopefully, you are reading this book out of a desire to bring more definition to your life.

The model for the Benedictine monastic community was the family. The head was called abbot, which means father, and served as the father figure for the other monks. The monks all addressed each other as brother and sought to treat each other as members of a single family, despite having come from very diverse backgrounds. This concept also transferred well to monastic houses for women, where the head became known as an abbess and everyone else addressed each other as sister.

The daily life of each monastery revolved around times of communal prayer. The monks gathered eight times a day for prayer. Matins (the office of readings) was held at midnight,

Lauds was at 3 A.M., Prime was at 6 A.M., Terce was at 9 A.M. and was followed by a mass. At noon, the monks prayed the office of Sext and moved to the midday meal. None came at 3 P.M. and was followed by outside labor in the farm or garden, as well as by housekeeping work. Evening prayer, Vespers, was prayed at 6 P.M. and Compline ended the day at 9 P.M. Additionally, they read the entire book of Psalms once a month and a chapter of the Rule each day. Monasteries today vary their schedules somewhat, and in most monasteries, educational work, retreat programs, and other endeavors have replaced the manual labor of farming. However, most still follow the structure and guide-lines set forth by Benedict.

At its essence, the Rule of St. Benedict is an effort to main-tain moderation in all things. He sought to cultivate in his monks "the simplicity of a life lived in common, reticence in speech, humble obedience to a spiritual master, the willingness to allow personal ambition and career to be set aside for the good of the community, work and prayer, and a discipline known as Lectio Divina" (3–4). Lectio Divina is a specialized method for the study of Scripture followed by a meditation on its meaning.

If you think about it, few Christians today live within a particular structure or discipline. They just try to attend their church and make their way through the trap-filled maze of daily life. Because many have tended to compartmentalize their faith from other aspects of life, their faith does not automatically guide decision making in those areas. When faced with a moral dilemma, our faith may not be able to speak as loudly as other aspects of our lives, like ego, desire, or guilt. But the problem goes far beyond moral dilemmas. If faith is compartmentalized and neglected, it cannot speak loudly and clearly to us when we are faced with questions about career, marital struggles, child rearing, community involvement, recreation, helping others, or standards of living. These all end up being addressed in a haphazard and arbitrary manner where things like ego, family of origin issues, or selfishness may be the loudest voices speaking. If faith is not allowed to speak to these areas in one's life, then what can it speak to? If you picture the image that is often used in cartoons where there is a little angel sitting on one shoulder and a little devil sitting on the other as you wrestle with a major decision, a more accurate picture would have the angel be far smaller and quieter than the little devil. The goal of a structure like the Rule of St. Benedict is to help create an environment where the angel is larger and more easily heard and where God can speak clearly in any situation. Therefore, let's look at some of the key features of Benedict's Rule and see how you may be able to apply it to your own daily life.

The first word of Benedict's Rule is, "Listen." This is the key to Benedictine spirituality. Learning how to listen to God speak throughout the course of normal events on average days is key so that the monk can see each moment of every day as a vital piece of the ongoing relationship with God. To listen is to recognize that God is the one who speaks wisdom and love, not us. To listen is to recognize that it is we who learn from God and not the other way around. To listen is to leave the thoughts of our minds and the distractions of our days behind as we listen to the very voice of love speak into our souls. Nothing else meaningful can happen on the spiritual journey unless one first learns how to listen.

The second sentence of the Rule states:

Receive willingly and carry out effectively
    your loving father's advice,
        that by the labor of obedience
        you may return to Him
            from whom you have departed
            by the sloth of disobedience." (13)

The fundamental assumption of Christianity is that God created the world to reflect his goodness and majesty, but that life has been corrupted. In looking at the struggles of our own lives, we can see the price each of us pays for this disobedience to God's intended order for creation. By listening, we hear God speak; by hearing God speak, we are shown the way back from our darkness to God's light; and by knowing the way back, we can meaningfully undertake the labor of obedience to return to God. In committing to this, we are called to renounce our own will and, as Benedict describes, "do battle under the Lord Jesus Christ, the true King, and [take] up the strong, bright weapons of obedience." (13).

Benedict established his Rule to organize his monks in a manner very different from a group called the Sarabaites. This form of monasticism was very popular before his time. In it, monks had no specific Rule to adhere to, they had no abbot to be accountable to, and they had full discretion over how to use the fruits of their labors. Other credible Christian writers saw them as being undisciplined, of questionable moral standards, and of dubious spiritual integrity. Benedict noted, "Their law is the desire for self-gratification: whatever enters their minds or appeals to them, that they call holy; what they dislike, they regard as unlawful" (22). Immersed in the "anything goes" culture of the Roman Empire, the Sarabaites tried to find a way to bring spiritual blessings to what was little more than the prevailing cultural values of the day. In reflecting on what passes for "spirituality" in the postmodern culture of today, one cannot help but wonder if we are surrounded by Sarabaites ourselves! It is as if we were to sit and decide what we want to do about a particular matter using our own reason and desires and then offer a prayer asking God to bless what we have decided on our own to do without any meaningful consultation with God (which, if you think about it, sounds a bit too much like many church committee meetings). The path of Benedictine spirituality is the exact opposite! It is one where we wait silently to hear what God is calling us to do and then, out of reverent obedience, ask God to give us the strength and fortitude to carry out his will. Perhaps this is why we see so many people in the early twenty-first century refer to themselves as "spiritual" instead of "religious." This allows for the warm and fuzzy feelings of being a "good and decent" person in the eyes of God without having to deal with any requirements, accountability, or change in lifestyle. They are able to maintain the values of a decadent society and feel they have God's blessings. It allows them to think that they have a meaningful spiritual life without having to do any of the work to really have one.

There is an enormous point to be made here. This kind of discernment does not mean that we just sit for a minute, get a feeling of what God wants us to do, and then run with that feeling. Far too many people have done this to their own destruction! It usually means that they, like the Sarabaites, are following their own inclinations and rationalizations. First John 4:1 warns us to "test the spirits" because there are so many false prophets and prophecies in the world. When we feel we have a word from God, it needs to be shared with others to see if they agree it is from God. One's pastor or priest, the endorsement of the church, and other sources are essential if we are to avoid falling into the trap of trying to put God's voice to our own desires! I have seen numerous instances where people were tempted to make rash decisions based on the emotional reactivity of the moment, but who, when they sought the counsel and advice of trusted friends, allowed cooler heads to prevail and followed a better path.

The human capacity for self-delusion is limitless! Human reason is a powerful tool, but it can all too easily be used to rationalize any form of bad behavior at all. The motivation that drives us to obedience to God only needs to be shifted a little bit in order to drive us to disobey. Also, the passion that drives us to do good for others only needs to be shifted a little bit in order for us to use that same passion to destroy. A big part of the problem for many is that they are unable to distinguish between the voices of God, the devil, and ourselves, and therefore risk making terrible decisions. If we want something badly enough, when we hear the devil's voice in prayer telling us that we deserve whatever it is we really think we want or need, we will be desperate to believe that we are really hearing the voice of God. This quickly leads to disappointment and heartache. Only through experience and through the testing of the spirits can we learn to distinguish the voices, and this is something that we cannot learn alone. The community of faith is essential for this learning process!

When the commandant of the Auschwitz concentration camp was on trial at Nuremberg after World War II, he was asked if he ever personally profited from the prisoners. His reply was an indignant, "What kind of person do you think I am?" Somehow, even though he ran a place for which the sole purpose was the murder of innocent people on an industrial scale, he still found a way to believe that he was a person of honor and integrity. Even after the war ended, he still could not see himself as anything but a noble officer in the army who would not take undue advantage of his prisoners. Though an extreme example, we all run the risk of fooling ourselves into believing whatever we want to about ourselves: "A person may think their own ways are right, but the Lord weighs the heart" (Prov. 21:2).

Keys to the Rule

In Benedict's Rule, some of the key themes that can apply to any Christian living today are humility, obedience, prayer, seeing the presence of God in daily life, discipline, and dealing with the danger of a compartmentalized life. It is important to consider each of these themes in turn.

Humility

At the absolute center of the life of a Benedictine is humility. To give up one's free will, to surrender one's life to God, and to follow wherever the journey leads is the ultimate act of humility. For Benedict, humility centered on obedience to God in all things, which is lived out through obedience to one's abbot, through putting the needs of others before his own, and in cultivating both love and patience toward all. In chapter 7 of the Rule, he describes twelve attributes of humility. They are:

1. Always keep God first.
2. Do not focus on what you want, but on what God wants.

3. Submit yourself to obey the Abbot as God's representative to the monastery.
4. Be patient and quiet when faced with injustice. Endure everything without growing weary or giving up.
5. Confess all evil thoughts. Do not let them fester in your mind.
6. Be content with everything and do not think your work is better than that of anyone else.
7. Do not place yourself higher than anyone. Think of yourself as the lowest in the group not just in actions, but in thoughts as well.
8. Do nothing that goes against the Rule or against the example of the elders.
9. Stay silent and do not speak unless someone asks you to.
10. Do not be quick to laugh at others. [Frivolity was seen as a bad quality among monks.]
11. When you speak, be gentle and serious. Do not be "noisy" in what you say.
12. Humility must be in both heart and appearance.

The importance of humility is that it ensures the Benedictine maintains a proper perspective on who God is and on who the believer is. It is through a proper understanding of and living with humility that has the power to limit the destructive influence of the ego and its desire to continually repeat the Original Sin of wanting to be in control of life and to think you have the power of God. This is not self-loathing, or a fake self-deprecation; it is a matter of perspective. Or, as has been often said, true humility is not about thinking less of yourself, it is about thinking about yourself less.

Obedience

Obedience to God is not blindly following a set of rules. This insults human intelligence and defeats the whole point of God giving human beings free will. True obedience is voluntarily submitting oneself to a relationship with God on God's terms. Some, who hold the values of our prevailing culture today, try to argue that submitting oneself to another, by definition, requires at least a small degree of destruction of the self. They argue that perfect freedom and perfect free will requires that nothing inhibit the full and free expression of the self. To submit to God or anyone is seen as a violation of the ideals of individualism and a display of "intolerance" against individual expression.

Though this argument may be consistent when seen within the context of postmodern thought, it is little more than another attempt to bless what already is, rather than an attempt to grow beyond the ordinary or to find a deeper meaning in life. For example, to become a concert pianist, one must spend endless hours playing the scales, doing rote work, and developing skill within a highly structured framework. It is only in mastery of the basics that the true artistic individuality of the pianist can find expression. To argue that one needs complete freedom from structure in order to be a truly artistic pianist would obviously be silly. The result would be little more than a person banging futilely on piano keys and making a terrible noise. It is out of the discipline of structure, playing the scales for hours and hours, that the pianist can eventually gain the skill to play with artistic freedom. There are many other instances where this is true.

A kung fu student submits to the skill of the sifu, the gymnast submits to the skill of the instructor, the artist submits to the understanding of the master, the academic submits to the experience of the professor, the driving student submits to the knowledge of the instructor, and so on. In none of these cases is the student lost or destroyed by the relationship. In every case, if the teacher is a good one, the student will flourish, grow, and thrive. In each case, the goal is for the student to reach his or her full potential. The same is true in faith. With God as the teacher, the goal is for each believer to reach the full potential in this life that God has given them. The basic and routine work that consumes so much time and energy is not pointless drudgery or cruel indoctrination; it is the work of defining a context and developing ability, which together lead to true freedom.

Obedience to God starts with a decision to enter into a relationship with God and to make the journey to wholeness that God calls us to. This requires complete trust in God! We are believing that God knows where we need to go and how to get us there, and we are choosing to give up our time, energy, and resources to follow that path because it is one that will lead us where we need to go. Of course, this is easier said than done. A fundamental understanding of life for Christians is that God created each of us on purpose and for a purpose. There is a specific reason why God has created each of us, and each of us has a specific reason for existence. Isn't that amazing? In those dark moments that everyone experiences, there is often a feeling of uselessness, of being unwanted, and of being unloved. Yet each life serves a precious and important part in God's plan! In other words, we each possess a God-shaped hole in our hearts, and we will never know true happiness until that hole is filled by an ongoing and healthy relationship with God.

With this in mind, what then was the true sin of Adam and Eve? The answer is that they did not want the relationship with God; they wanted the power to be equal to God. When the serpent tempted Eve, the temptation was that eating of the Tree of the Knowledge of Good and Evil would give her not only understanding, but an understanding that would make her like God. There are two things that are compelling about this story. The first is that Adam and Eve were given the choice of living in paradise, so long as they did so on God's terms; or to live on their own terms and know suffering and death. The point of the story is that they chose death. The finite wanted to be infinite. The two who were limited by time and space wanted to be freed from those constraints. How did they come to believe it was possible? The answer is human ego. The serpent flattered their desire to have the same greatness as God and clouded their understanding of what their relationship with God was meant to be. Today, our whole civilization is built on feeding the human ego. This has been profoundly destructive. The reason this matters is that it is the same choice that almost all people in history have made. Most people would choose a life of suffering and pain, so long as they can live it on their own terms; rather than live in relationship with God and know peace. We all say we want the world to be a better place, but too few of us are willing to change ourselves to help get it there. Of this, Richard John Neuhaus wrote that we end up being "herds of independent minds marching towards moral oblivion with Frank Sinatra's witless boast on our lips, 'I Did It My Way'" (quoted in Colson, 376).

The other compelling image from the Garden of Eden is the two trees. Adam and Eve had the freedom to eat from the Tree of Life and to live forever, but they instead chose to eat from the Tree of the Knowledge of Good and Evil and to suffer death. What is it about human nature that causes us to do this? We all want to live forever but are willing to sacrifice eternal life, or even go so far as to ignore it when it is freely offered, in order to live the way we want to for today. This point is so profound that it is worth spending significant time in prayer with, because what lies at the heart of it is what keeps each one of us from willingly submitting to God in obedience.

Sadly, a third aspect of human nature that Eden teaches us is just how quickly the negative aspects of human nature emerge. As soon as Adam and Eve discovered what they had done, they hid from God, and they tried to pass the blame. If you believe that God is all-knowing, then the idea of trying to hide from God is silly. Yet, this is what they did and what we often try to do. We commit our own personal sins with the vague hope that God will not notice. Passing the blame is just as juvenile. Adam blamed Eve, and Eve blamed the serpent. It seems to be hard-wired into human nature to be dishonest about our mistakes. What was God's response? Humanity was expelled from the Garden because the relationship had been broken. Also, the Tree of Life needed to be sealed off because if they ate from it at that point, they would have been stuck in the fallen state forever. Something else had to be done to restore the broken relationship, and it did not fully happen until the death of Jesus on the cross at Calvary, which is why the cross is sometimes referred to as the "tree of life." It is through what happened on the wood of the cross that the damage of Eden was undone and eternal life is once again offered.

So, because humanity has chosen, and continues to choose, to follow its own way instead of God's, the relationship we were each created to be in continues to be broken. The journey of faith is one where we learn to let go of our unhealthy desire for control and seek to restore the relationship to its intended state. In essence, it is to return to the state it was once in at Eden. This requires a deep and serious obedience that centers on the surrender of our free will to God and trusting that God has a plan. There is no other way.

Here is a serious issue to ponder. If you feel you have made progress in surrendering to God as you make your way through this life, then consider these questions: How close to Eden do you currently feel? Do you feel the bliss of complete obedience and a fulfilling relationship with God? Or is the struggle to surrender an ongoing one? Do you know what needs to be done, but are procrastinating? Are you, like St. Augustine shortly before his conversion, praying, "Grant me chastity and continence, but not yet" (152)? Being able to honestly answer these questions and to take action based on those answers is an important step in spiritual growth.

Prayer

Another key to Benedictine spirituality is the recognition that prayer comes before work. In chapter 43, Benedict instructs that when the bell that calls monks to prayer rings, the monks are to drop everything else and cease all work. The monks are then to go to the chapel "with haste" to participate in prayer time. It is of essential importance for them to know that they are not farmers, herdsmen, cooks, or writers who happen to take time to pray. Instead, they are people who pray first and foremost. Prayer time does not interrupt work; work interrupts prayer time. Everything else must flow from their prayer lives, so all of their work must be in response to their time in prayer. This is not an intellectual idea or thought. It is a worldview question that must remain in the center of daily life in order to constantly remind the monks what comes first. As Benedict writes, "Let nothing, therefore, be put before the Work of God" (43.3) and this means that nothing can take priority over prayer in the life of the monastery and of a Benedictine. Think about this in terms of your own life. Are you a physician, a clerk, or a student who happens to be a Christian, or are you a Christian who happens to be a physician, a clerk, or a student? How does your life reflect this reality? Is it done through shaping your life to fit your faith, or do you find yourself trying to shape your faith to fit your life?

The challenge many Christians face today is that in the compartmentalized lives we live, we do not spend our days in constant prayer. We see Sunday worship as the time for this. I have heard people go so far as to say, "God only asks for one hour a week." What a lie! God expects every hour of every day. Prayer cannot be compartmentalized to the point where it only takes place at church, or in saying prayers at bedtime, or in grace before a meal. These are all wonderful times to pray, but they ought not serve as the only times! To "pray without ceasing" as Paul describes it in 1 Thessalonians 5:17 (NKJV), is to make the whole day a conversation with God. Let your thoughts and your reflections be a talk with God. Talk with God while driving, walking the dog, waiting in a line, standing in an elevator, shopping in a store, reading a book, or enjoying a beautiful scene of nature. You will feel God's presence more strongly when God becomes a part of your everyday life. Short prayers can happen spontaneously and anywhere. You must also make time for more meaningful and specific times of daily prayer and worship. Other aspects of our lives should be seen as interruptions to prayer, not the other way around.

Chapters 8 through 18 of the Rule offer specific guidelines detailing how to conduct the various prayer services throughout the day. The many specific directions indicate that the services were important encounters with God, and that God deserves our best when we come before him. For example, in writing about the weekday morning office in chapter 13, Benedict writes,

> Let Psalm 66 be said without an antiphon and somewhat slowly, as on Sunday, in order that all may be in time for Psalm 50, which is to be said with an antiphon. After that let two other psalms be said according to custom, namely: on Monday Psalms 5 and 35, on Tuesday Psalms 42 and 56, on Wednesday Psalms 63 and 64, on Thursday Psalms 87 and 89, on Friday Psalms 75 and 91, and on Saturday Psalm 142 and the canticle from Deuteronomy, which is to be divided into two sections each terminated by a "Glory be to the Father." (60–61)

Despite this specificity, and despite all of the details surrounding all other gatherings of prayer, Benedict does not want his monks to get lost in the details of the prayer times. He offers this caveat in chapter 18:

> We strongly recommend, however, that if this distribution of the Psalms is displeasing to anyone, he should

arrange them otherwise, in whatever way he considers better, but taking care in any case that the Psalter with its full number of 150 Psalms be chanted every week and begun again every Sunday at the Night Office. (69–70)

The care and specificity of Benedict's instructions are not arbitrary. They are meant to foster intentionality and a deliberate approach to the work of worship. It is to be neither haphazard nor spontaneous. This only makes sense! To engage in any important task and to do it well, a person must spend time preparing for it. It would be foolhardy to approach a matter of great importance and seriousness without thought or planning. Think about how you would approach an interview for a job you really want. Would you plan your questions and answers and seek to show the interviewer your seriousness, or would you give the matter little attention and just show up? What about an important exam? Would you spend time studying and preparing, or just show up and hope for the best? What about an important business presentation where the outcomes will have a profound effect on your career? Do you spend time preparing the presentation and thinking through the questions that may arise, or do you show up without any thought or preparation?

The answers to these questions are self-evident. Yet if the answer to these is clear, then what does it say about our understanding of God and the importance of who God is if we just show up for community worship without having given the matter any thought or preparation? Are we truly giving God our best? Are we truly making a statement that we believe God is the almighty and all-powerful creator of the universe? Are we honestly saying that we believe God is worthy of our best? Or are we assuming that God will be grateful for whatever table scraps we happen to bring?

Benedict understood the need to give God our best, but he sought to balance this need with the caution that we do not want to make the structure the end in itself. The structure is just the means by which we approach God in a proper and reverent manner. Therefore, even though it is of the utmost importance that we approach worship with seriousness, reverence, and dignity, we do not want to focus all of our attention on the structure itself. This would undoubtedly be a case of the tail wagging the dog! The specifics of how to approach worship are important, but they are not the focus. Because of this, they can be altered (as described in chapter 18 of the Rule) in order to help better serve their purpose, which is the worship of Almighty God.

Seeing the Presence of God in Daily Life

Another significant aspect of Benedictine life was the call to be mindful of the presence of the holy in everything related to daily living. Nothing existed apart from God and nothing was to be done apart from God. For example, in addressing the work of the cellarer (the individual who provided food and drinks to others in the monastery): "Let him regard all of the utensils of the monastery and its whole property as if they were the sacred vessels of the altar. Let him not think that he may neglect anything" (83). This is partly a matter of stewardship because we should see nothing as being truly our own and should always look to everything we have as things we have been entrusted by God to care for. It is also partly a matter of working to end the false separation of faith and life that existed both in Benedict's day as well as in our own. To truly live in the presence of God calls us to see God present everywhere we go and in everything we do. Preparing food for others to eat is not just a task that one should look forward to completing, and washing cups after a meal is not merely a drudgery of a task that needs to be done. Benedict calls for us to treat simple things like plates and cups as though they were sacred items for use in the most holy of moments. Serving others is not a chore that someone happens to be stuck with, but is rather an opportunity to serve Christ himself. When asked how she could go through the rubbish- and sewage-filled gutters of Calcutta to look for the dying and diseased people and bring them to her center where they could die with dignity, Mother Teresa said that she saw the very face of Jesus in each person she helped. We too need to see Jesus in all we do and in all whom we serve. If our personal Rule for Life does not inculcate these virtues, we have missed something very important in life!

Does this seem a little extreme? If so, think about how you currently view Jesus in your daily life. Do you just have an intellectual understanding that he is always present, or is his presence part of your daily living? If you really feel God's daily presence, what has changed as a result of this experience? Most people live daily life on one plane of existence and experience Sunday worship on another plane of existence, and the two seldom, if ever, intersect. In chapter 35 of the Rule, Benedict instructs that all monks should spend time working in the kitchen, because of the important spiritual rewards that service to others brings. The reason for this is that, unlike tending a garden or caring for animals in the barn, kitchen duty is one where the focus is clearly on serving others. It cannot be done alone, and it does not allow for solitary pleasures. It is a menial, gritty, and hard job that is focused solely on service to others. When one can see God in dirty pots and pans and find joy in the smallest kitchen task, then one has learned about how to sense God's holy presence in the midst of daily life.

One of the best-known examples of living like this comes from the profound little book called *The Practice of the Presence of God* by Brother Lawrence. He was a lay brother in a Carmelite monastery in Paris in the seventeenth century. He was so poorly educated that the only job they could find for him in the monastery was in the kitchen, where he spent twenty-five years of his adult life cleaning up after meals. However, he had such a serenity and love for God that he attracted the attention of others both inside and outside the monastery. Upon his death, another monk wrote of his spiritual life, attitude toward work, and love for others. This book is so profound that it has sold over twenty million copies and has been continually in print for the past three hundred years! In it, we hear of how Brother Lawrence saw every moment of every day as a continual conversation with God. Since God is everywhere, every moment is spent living in the presence of God. When he scrubbed pots, he did not see it as mere drudgery—it was time to spend praising God and in conversation with God. When he mopped floors, it was not a thankless chore—it was a time to share his thoughts and feelings with God. Every aspect of every day became part of his prayer life. He saw nothing as trivial, and he believed that God was actually interested in even the smallest details of his life. For him, the times the monastery gathered for community prayer were no different than when he was working alone in the kitchen. It was all filled with prayer and praise. As he said, "We ought not be weary of doing little things for the love of God, who regards not the greatness of the work, but the love with which it is performed."

Discipline

Another important part of life in a monastery centers on what is to be done when monks violate the Rule. For Benedict, one of the most important parts of monastic life is to live together as family; therefore the most significant punishment that can be meted out to disobedient monks is to be given a "time out" from the community. He writes that appropriate punishment is to make monks eat by themselves apart from the others, to have them work alone, or to bar them from community prayer time. If they engage in behavior that is hurtful to the community, then an experience of being separated from the community can serve as a reminder of not only how important the community is, but how much spiritual and emotional suffering arises, both when one does something to harm the life of the community, as well as when one is separated from community. In Amish circles, the practice of "shunning" serves a similar purpose. When your identity is defined to a large degree by the community you are a part of, alienation from that community is a serious punishment. To a lesser degree, the same is done when children are given a "time out" from their toys, friends, or family. The isolation quickly reinforces the value of the family (or their toys) and helps the repentant to learn not to take it so for granted, and not to so blithely hurt it again.

This sort of discipline may seem alien to our culture, for ours is a culture that prizes individual freedom and does not clearly understand the nature of responsibility. It is very common for someone to commit to being a part of the life of a church, but as soon as something happens they do not agree with, they abandon the community. I have seen this countless times in churches, and yet I have never seen someone admit that it really is nothing more than an "I'm taking my ball and going home" moment. Instead, the departure is always wrapped up in the language of the church not being a "real" church, or the pastor not being Christian enough, or the person not being "fed" anymore. Since churches have no meaningful way to enforce community, people are under no pressure to do the hard work of making community meaningful, and "church hopping" has become an ever more common phenomenon.

In the eyes of some, discipline is seen as little more than arbitrary or unfair punishment that does little to help the individual being punished and, in fact, can do untold damage instead. It is important here to make a distinction between discipline and abuse. Abuse comes when discipline is used arbitrarily, capriciously, or out of a desire by the one dispensing the punishment to satisfy their own desire to inflict pain. In this instance, no good can come of the punishment, and it is in fact harmful to the one on the receiving end.

The discipline that Benedict talks about is a very different phenomenon. Just as child psychologists talk about the need for children to have structure and discipline in their lives in order to grow up emotionally and psychologically healthy, Benedict saw that his monks needed consequences for going beyond what is allowed by the structure of the Rule. When one willfully engages in behavior that hurts others, social consequences are intended to help serve as a reminder of the value and importance of community, as well as to offer a meaningful way back into the community. In Benedictine discipline, the goal is always restoration, healing, and deeper community—not punishment.

I know that advocating for church discipline is a losing cause, but we can at least make the case for staying with community, even when the going gets tough. When we commit to community, we commit to a relationship. This means we remain committed when we do not get our own way. It means we accept that we may be wrong when we adamantly feel we are right; we commit to working with people we may not particularly like; and we stay, even when we want to run away. This is immensely difficult to do, and I confess that I have only had mixed success doing this in my own life. However, I can honestly say that I am making an effort to do it. The learning process can be a long, slow one.

Commitment to community over the long haul brings us through the whole range of human emotions, including joy, anger, love, disdain, pride, embarrassment, serenity, agitation, and confusion. The benefits of commitment to community are innumerable. We develop a sense that we belong to something bigger than ourselves, we learn to work through difficult relationships, and we learn how to say "I am sorry" instead of running away. These are powerful lessons that cannot be learned any other way. That is why Jesus wanted his followers to gather as the church rather than to practice the faith on their own. One might go so far as to suggest that church is practice for heaven, because these are all things we need to learn before we get to heaven.

Dealing with the Danger of a Compartmentalized Life

The concepts described in this chapter can be difficult to grasp for people who struggle to follow the Christian way. Given the fragmentation of our lives, it is hard to consider the notion that there is one overriding thought that must govern and guide all of the different things we do and participate in. It is hard to imagine that the difficulties of community life are an essential part of individual formation. If we are accustomed to compartmentalizing everything and have devoted countless hours to maintaining the separation of those things (whether work, spouse, children, hobbies, faith, church, community involvement, politics, or other entertainment), then it may be hard to conceptualize setting one thing as the center of our lives and then having everything else revolve around it. After all, how do we take time at our jobs to pray? How can we be expected to give up our music interests if they focus on values and priorities that contradict those of our faith? When life is so busy, how can we be expected to give time to serving the church? Besides, doesn't this level of commitment seem just a little cult-like? Doesn't it mean that we have to give up everything that we like about being ourselves and replace it with dour, dowdy, dull, and delirious tedium? Who or what is to really determine what the new "me" is to look like? And furthermore, if we are going to try to follow this and then fail, does our failure just prove us to be little more than the hypocrites that so many people think Christians are anyway?

The answers to these questions are not nearly as complicated as we may try to make them out to be. The challenge is to always focus on deepening our relationship with God. The challenge is to start to bring God to other aspects of our lives, which is a process that takes time and effort, and includes mistakes. The issue is not so much falling into line according to the dictates of some morals police. The issue is falling in love with God and following what ensues from that. It is first about learning how to love God, then about how to see God's presence in daily occurrences (i.e., the beauty of nature or the humor of a moment), about learning how to serve others out of our love for God and not out of a desire for reward, about learning how to see Jesus in the face of others, and about learning how to love others as an expression of our love for Jesus.

Other stuff will come as part of this process. For example, seeing God's presence in daily life will help eliminate our doubts about God's existence or goodness. Learning to serve others will teach us to address our own selfishness. Learning to love others will address our tendencies to use other people as means to our own ends. Seeing Jesus in others will change the way we hear our music. Letting faith guide every decision helps us to see better the beauty and holiness of God's creation. Falling desperately in love with God gives us the desire to follow the discipline of a biblical lifestyle. Even though we may think we are too busy to try any of this, the truth is that our busyness is more of an excuse than a legitimate reason. The great discovery of choosing the Christian path is not that it is dreary and joyless but that it is the path to joy, serenity, and fulfillment.

Choosing the Christian way is not so much an issue of joining the army where the rules must be learned, superiors obeyed unconditionally, and loyalty to the institution trumps all personal thoughts and interests. Choosing the Christian way is more like falling in love with someone. Little is known or understood about the other early on, but there is an incredible sense of joy and attraction. Over time, as the relationship deepens and the love strengthens, the interests of the two lovers come together, and their joy spills over into all aspects of their lives. When together, they experience bliss; when apart, their thoughts continually remain on one another whether they are at work, at home, and even when with other friends. Just like in a deepening relationship, the early years are spent with lots of late nights spent talking and lots of new discoveries being made. And, as the relationship matures, less needs to be said and joy is found just in being in each other's company.

The journey of spiritual growth is similar. Love is the key. "Whoever does not love does not know God, because God is love" (1 John 4:8). Chapter 72 of the Rule could serve as a code of life for anyone today:

> Just as there is an evil zeal of bitterness which separates from God and leads to hell, so there is a good zeal which separates from vices and leads to God and to life everlasting. This zeal, therefore, the monks should practice with the most fervent love. Thus they should anticipate one another in honor; most patiently endure one another's infirmities, whether of body or of character; vie in paying obedience to one another—no one following what he considers useful to himself, but rather what benefits another; tender the charity of brotherhood chastely; fear God in love; love their Abbot with a sincere and humble charity; prefer nothing whatever to Christ. And may he bring us all together to life everlasting! (98–99)

This chapter calls the monks to not just be nice to each other, but to really strive to put each other before themselves. It calls them to love those whom they would not ordinarily choose to love, to help those whom they do not necessarily want to help, and to raise up those whom they would prefer to drag down. It also calls them not to help others when it is useful for their own needs, but when it is beneficial for the other, when there is nothing to be gained personally. It is a wonderful sentiment; one that comes straight from the Gospels, but one that can be incredibly difficult to try to live by.

Here is a two-minute exercise that illustrates the point. Just think about someone who drives you crazy. It doesn't matter why they do, just that they do. It could be a relative with crazy ideas about life, a coworker with an annoying habit, a neighbor who you see as nothing less than a total nemesis, or any of the other people you come in contact with regularly. Now, how can you look at that person with a genuine sense of love, and how can you act in a manner to best help that person? How can you genuinely celebrate that person's successes and overlook their weaknesses? What can you do in the next week that will help that person and bring absolutely no benefit to yourself? Unless you are one of the truly rare people in this world, you will be able to come up with someone, and this little exercise will actually be painful. If you feel pain, then you get the point. This is how hard the path to unconditional love of your neighbor really is, and it is precisely what Christians are called to manifest in their daily lives.

Another piece of this is to avoid the trap of focusing on the failings of others so that we can disregard our own. In twelve-step programs, leaders talk about how you must focus on your own "inventory" (exploring, naming, and working on the things in your own life that need to be changed) and about how you must never take the "inventory" of others (naming what is wrong in their lives and what they must do to correct this). Though it is always easier to see what is wrong in others than it is to see what is wrong in our own lives, by focusing our attention on others, we make two key mistakes. First, we avoid the work we must be doing on our own lives. Second, and perhaps even more important, in taking the inventory of another, we assume that we know what is wrong and what is best for the other person. It takes a big ego to make these assumptions! You can *never* fully know what is going on with another person, and you can *never* be sure that you are offering the best advice. Each person has her own story and must live her own life. To judge is to engage in great spiritual peril (see Matt. 7:1). Therefore, it is safer, more humble, more honest, and more healthy, to focus our attention on our own work and to let other people work with God on their own faults.

Developing a Rule for Life

All of this may sound good for a bunch of monks who live cloistered in a monastery. Given that living in a monastery is not a practical option for most of us, what can we do as an alternative? We can take the principles Benedict used for his monasteries and develop a personal Rule for Life that incorporates them. We can develop a written guide that can help us to remember what defines our lives, what our priorities are, and where the boundaries are. We can use a compass to draw a circle around our lives that then leaves no doubt as to what is included within our lives and what is to be left outside.

Developing a Rule for Life can be done in three steps, the goal of which is both to establish the parameters for daily living and to quantify the spiritual disciplines that will be followed on a consistent basis. **The first step is to define your understanding of life.** This includes naming a life verse from Scripture, stating your specific life purpose, identifying your spiritual gifts, naming the specific reasons you love Jesus, identifying what you are most committed to, and naming who needs your love the most. The reason for this step is to help you go through a deliberate process to name your core values—things everyone has in their lives, but which few people ever stop to consider or even identify.

The second step is to define the spiritual disciplines that will structure the habits of daily life. A meaningful life does not happen by accident. It requires deliberate and focused effort. It centers on identifying and committing to developing a daily prayer discipline, a Bible study regimen, making a small group commitment, maintaining an intercessory prayer list, naming what you do for fun, naming what you do for your family, naming what you do for your church, naming what you do for your community, identifying what sacrifices you are making for the sake of the gospel, and naming what personal weaknesses you are working on. By doing this, you are creating a pattern of behavior that will help you to develop a spiritual vitality that will guide your life to fulfill its purpose.

The third step is to take the information gathered in the first two steps and to identify the trajectory that God is leading your life across. This includes naming your life's purpose (as you currently understand it), and setting a series of goals that will help you to fulfill that purpose. Taking this step includes participating in a process of identifying your passions and personality traits, and being able to name your call from God in a single sentence. The next step is to set one-year, five-year, and long-term goals for growth toward that calling. The process is completed by committing to at least an annual process of reflection on and revising your goals. This takes place through having quiet days of reflection or by participating in a retreat. By engaging in an intentional process of evaluation, you ensure that you are living your life deliberately and seriously, not merely as a reaction to daily events.

All of this may sound like a lot, but life has a lot of moving parts! Proverbs 29:18a states, "where there is no vision, the people perish" (KJV). Most people have little vision for their lives other than to react to the immediate needs and demands of the moment. The series of exercises just described offers a fascinating and enlightening journey into what it means to truly live while we walk on this earth for the few short years that we are here. Chapters Five, Six, and Seven will explore each of these steps in greater detail, and our concluding goal will be to help you fill out the Rule for Life chart that is available at the book's website (www.truepilgrim.com). As you work on these, be sure to have fun with the process!

Questions for Reflection

1. The first word in the Rule of St. Benedict is "listen." Does your prayer life include listening to God? If so, how? If not, how is that a problem in your prayer life?

2. Three of the key aspects of a well-ordered life are humility, obedience, and prayer. How do you intentionally work on each of these in your own Christian formation?

3. Name the last few times you saw God at work in ordinary occurrences in daily life. What impact did these instances have on you?

4. What was your experience when you did the two-minute exercise (described in this chapter) to show love for someone who drives you crazy? What did you do that was solely for that person's benefit?

5. What do you think is the benefit of a personal Rule for Life? What worries you about developing one?

5

How to Develop a Rule for Life, Part I
Defining Your Life

"Holiness is not the luxury of the few
but a simple duty for you and me.
So, let us be holy as our Father in heaven is holy."

—Mother Teresa of Calcutta, "And You, Who Do You Say That I Am?"

The success of the Rule of Benedict for over fifteen hundred years illustrates the importance of having a structured and disciplined approach to spiritual formation. For most of human history, economics and limited mobility severely curtailed the amount of time people had for anything other than survival. If it took sixteen hours of hard work each day just to survive, that left little time for anything else. Today, life is very different. Our options are almost limitless in terms of travel, entertainment, education, activism, recreation, spiritual interest, and lifestyle. Anything goes, and everything is for sale. The moral norms that anchored Western civilization for so many centuries have given way to a free-for-all where anything is possible and everything is seen as good. This is why it has become especially important to be careful to have a structure for how to live faith. If we try to follow God, while at the same time living immersed in the surrounding culture, the culture will quickly erode the faith into something tepid and sterile. Or, as we saw with the Sarabaites in the last chapter, we may give in to the values of the society and try to legitimize them by wrapping them up in the language of faith.

The journey into wholeness cannot be accidental or an afterthought. It requires care and seriousness. For spontaneous types of people, this all may sound suffocating, but even if you do not wish to follow a Rule, completing the exercises in this chapter can still be an educational and enlightening experience. So please, stick with it! For people who like to be structured, this may be the perfect way to help you follow the old adage, "Plan your work and work your plan."

Building a Rule for Life

An important part of building a meaningful life is reaching the moment where we experience a Copernican change. Just as Copernicus sparked a revolution in astronomy when he showed that the earth revolved around the sun instead of the sun revolving around the earth, a spiritual Copernican change happens when we realize that God does not exist to serve our needs, but that we exist to serve God. This is the discovery that begins to undo the damage of Original Sin because it represents the moment where we realize that we are not the center of the universe. It marks the moment where we discover just how much bigger than us God really is and how, if we are to take this discovery seriously, we need to take God and God's call for us seriously.

Building a Rule for Life in today's world requires that we account for all of the complex components of daily living. These factors can be grouped into three general areas. These areas are (1) defining your life, (2) describing your disciplines, and (3) dreaming your goals. To define your life is to draw the circle that will delineate the boundaries within which you will live and beyond which you will not go. It also helps to identify your priorities and purpose in life. Being able to describe your disciplines is important because these are the conscious steps and actions that you commit to in order to follow God and stay true to your life's definition. Finally, dreaming about your goals is important because it identifies the trajectory that your life is pointing to. It shows your most important dreams and your desired destination in life. Together, these three facets create a coherent context within which you can live a devout Christian life. This chapter and the two following will walk you through each factor. Let's get started.

Defining Your Life

To define your life, it is important to be able to name the things that are most important to you. It is also important to be able to name your life's purpose, identify what gifts you possess, prioritize the commitments you have, and name who is most important to you in life. In other words, the Defining Your Life section structures your worldview.

Your Life's Purpose

Fundamental to the Christian life is the belief in the sanctity of life. Each person is seen as a precious child of God who has been made to reflect the very image of God. Over the past two thousand years, Christians have built orphanages, served the poor, built hospitals, ministered to those in prison, run schools, and done countless other works of charity because of this belief in the preciousness of life. Christian arguments against capital punishment and abortion both stem from this understanding of the value of life.

It is also out of this understanding of life that Christians develop an understanding of the purposefulness of life. This is the belief that each person is born on purpose, has certain experiences in life on purpose, and has a mission that God desires them to fulfill. No life is random or accidental. No life lacks meaning. Lives can and are quite often broken, damaged, or even lost, but this does not take away from the intentions of God for that life. After all, if you are made in the very image of God, then this is a holy and precious thing God has done, and all holy things of God do matter. This begs the question of how we can determine our life's purpose. You might think that life would be a lot easier if we had our purpose stamped on our rear ends at birth. As nice as this would seem to be, it would take too much away from the adventure of life. If we are to see life as a wonderful adventure of discovery and growth, then one of the most significant discoveries we can experience is the discovery of our purpose in life. One of the great joys of clergy is to be with people when they make the discovery of their purpose. It is a holy moment because you know that the person has had a profound encounter with God and will never be the same as a result of it. It is awesome stuff!

Our postmodern culture completely rejects this notion. It tries to argue that human existence is an accident of nature and that life has little or no inherent meaning. Postmodernism argues this because if life does have a purpose, then postmodernism would have to accept responsibility for living up to that purpose, which goes against the hedonistic underpinnings that strive for complete freedom from responsibility. The truth is that God made you on purpose and made you with a purpose. Discovering your purpose and finding out how God wants you to fulfill it is a powerful and holy experience!

There are as many possible life purposes as there are people. While it has long been accepted that clergy are "called by God" into ministry, it is far less common to hear everyone else talk about being called by God into the work they do in life. It is inaccurate to think that only those who are engaged in full-time church work are people that God has given a specific purpose to. It is also inaccurate to assume that your calling must also be your profession. Sometimes it is and sometimes it isn't. Stories abound of accountants whose purpose is to work with at-risk youth, doctors whose purpose is to lead the music in church, factory workers whose purpose is to shepherd a small group, engineers whose purpose is to teach young children, and salespeople whose purpose is to be a voice of encouragement to people facing significant crises. Career and calling are sometimes the same, or they can also be two very different things. A career helps you earn a living, while your calling helps you build a life. However, given how serious a life's purpose is, identifying it must be done with care.

The corporate world has taken the question of purpose very seriously in recent decades. Both companies and churches have worked to develop mission and vision statements as a way to focus sharply on what they will and will not be about. Once a statement has been defined, the next step is to look at everything already being done and measure those things against the statement. If existing activities support the mission, they are to be encouraged. If they go against it, they are to be discontinued, regardless of how popular they may be. The problem is that in far too many cases, this exercise has little effect. Many organizations do the work to develop the statement, but do not follow through in implementing it. They do not take the next step of measuring everything they do against what they claim they are all about in their vision or mission statement. In other words, they did not modify their worldview to fit the vision statement, and so in practice, the old worldview will continue unchanged and the vision statement will get filed in a cabinet.

If an individual is able to name a life purpose, then it only has lasting value if all activities and interests are measured against that purpose and appropriate action taken. We need to make an honest assessment of what is in alignment with our purpose and what moves against it; then, everything that moves against it needs to be dropped. If someone's life purpose is to help at-risk youth, it makes little sense to serve on a church finance committee, especially if the work of the committee takes the person away from their purpose of helping youth! The trap people fall into is one where they believe that any help or service to others is "good enough."

I once served a church where there was an average of eighty-five people attending each week, yet they had over a dozen committees and needed over one hundred and twenty people to fill all of the committee slots. This structure had been put into place decades before when the church had over a thousand members, and even though the demographics of the church had changed profoundly, the structure had not. This meant that the most active people in the church served on two or three committees simultaneously and felt that this was "good enough" for their spiritual well-being. However, they were so busy attending meetings that they could not find the time for adult education, Bible study, or small groups. So much effort went into keeping seats filled in the committees that the spiritual life of the community stagnated. What made the situation even worse was that people came to identify their committee roles as their spirituality. I once had a person tell me that his work on the Property Committee made up for the lack of a prayer life or engagement in spiritual disciplines. I guess he thought that God was more worried about the roof of the building and whether the grass was cut than he was about whether the committee member was developing into the person he had been created to become!

It is absolutely essential that we remember that God first created us to be in relationship with him. Once we are in that relationship and growing in it, we need to then engage in the work that God has called us to do. It is so important to remember that if your purpose is to evangelize individuals, you need to be engaged directly in evangelism; if it is to teach children, you need to teach; and if it is to help hurting people, you need to help them. It is important to always keep the main thing the main thing. If you can or desire to do more, that's fine, so long as it doesn't take away from your core purpose. If other work is taking you away from your purpose, then you have to honestly name it and gracefully release yourself from it. Additionally, if unhealthiness keeps you from achieving your purpose, then you have a profound and holy responsibility to work on it. If alcoholism or its effects are impeding you from your purpose, then you need to join AA or Al-Anon. If you struggle with working long hours in your profession and this becomes an impediment, it is important to find ways to set better boundaries for work time. If you are so obsessive-compulsive that people do not want to work with you, it is important to commit the time and energy to treat the problem so it stops impeding the work and relationships. There are so many things, both positive and negative, that impede spiritual growth and the fulfillment of a life purpose. Honesty about what they are and commitment to dealing with them are essential!

To identify your purpose, it is important to look at the things in your life that excite your imagination, the things you lie in bed thinking about at night, the things you seem especially gifted at. I had no idea I was called to be a teacher until I was working in my first church and realized that the highlight of my week was teaching the adult education Bible study class. Preparing for them was joyful, leading them was fun, and I would go home so energized that I would have trouble falling asleep. This did not happen to the same degree in any other aspect of my work in that parish. It was a wonderful discovery!

God has wired you in a manner that has equipped you to accomplish your purpose. Being an introvert or an extrovert, thinking systematically, being a teacher, having a knack for intercessory prayer, being a people person, being well organized, having a good memory for details, being able to lead others, being strongly intuitive, and a number of other similar traits all contribute to defining how God has wired you. Your task is to make a list and share it with others who can either confirm or honestly question what you have concluded.

Many people read about life purpose and immediately conclude that because they do not know their purpose, they must not have one. This is not true! If you are breathing, then God has a purpose for you on this earth. A course can help determine your purpose, spiritual direction can help, and working with a clergy person can help. It takes time and the help of others to discern your purpose, but be patient and be persistent!

Think about what gets you the most excited. What can keep you up at night, what creates the most satisfaction for you, what brings the most joy, and what makes the time go by the fastest for you? Your passion should be something that has always been present in your life, even if it has been unnamed. It should also be something that if you share it with a friend, they will not be surprised because they can already see it at work in your life.

Name your life's purpose or the process you will use to discover it:

_____

_____

_____

_____

Life Verse

A life verse is a verse or section of verses in the Bible that provides encouragement and guidance in a unique and spiritually significant manner. It is usually a statement that summarizes your understanding of God, defines what you understand your life to be, or offers encouragement to the specific challenges that you regularly endure. A person's life verse offers a unique perspective on the faith and life of that person. For example, a Methodist minister I know has John 3:17 as his verse: "For, God did not send his Son into the world to condemn the world, but to save the world through him." He sees this verse as important because he sees his primary function as a pastor to be one of helping people to find salvation through Jesus. I know someone who is deeply involved in Stephen Ministry (a program for training lay people to offer pastoral support for people facing significant crisis in their lives), and she uses Isaiah 6:8, which is a theme verse for the ministry: "Then I heard the voice of the Lord saying, 'Whom shall I send? And who will go for us?' And I said, 'Here am I. Send me!'" She identifies herself very strongly as a Stephen Minister, and her life is lived as an answer to God's call of who will go to those in need. I also know a philosophy teacher at a college who has a profoundly deep and rich spiritual life. She sees her goal as being one of showing atheists how illogical their lack of belief in God is. Her verse is Jeremiah 29:13: "You will seek me and find me when you seek me with all your heart." For a number of years, while engaged in pastoral ministry, my own life verse was 1 Corinthians 15:58: "Therefore, my beloved brethren, be steadfast, immovable, always abounding in the work of the Lord, knowing that your labor is not in vain in the Lord" (NKJV). When I shifted from pastoral work to academia, my verse changed to Psalm 131:2, to remind me of how much I do not know and of what my true goal in learning is: "But I have calmed and quieted myself, I am like a weaned child with its mother; like a weaned child I am content." This verse helped me keep my perspective as I risked getting swallowed up in the arcane theoretical work of academia.

You may know a verse or story from Scripture that comes back to you again and again. There may be one you have heard others quote that speaks directly to your heart every time you hear it. You may even have heard someone else share a life verse that you immediately thought applied to you. These are all okay! As long as it represents where you are or where you seek to go, how you choose it is not so important. What is important is to remember that life verses are special and should not be chosen haphazardly. They can also change as the circumstances of your life change.

A life verse needs to be something that arises out of a process of prayer and discernment. It is something that God needs to reveal because it is something that should continually offer spiritual nourishment. By taking the time to pray and to reflect on a life verse, we gain clarity into what God is calling us to as we walk this earth.

Name your life verse:

Spiritual Gifts

Spiritual gifts are the specific tools that God gives each person to fulfill his life's purpose. They do not define one's purpose, but they provide what a person needs to fulfill her purpose. If someone is wearing a tool belt that has a saw, a hammer, a level, nails, wood glue, and a tape measure, it would seem reasonable to assume that this person is a carpenter. If, on the other hand, the tool belt contained wire cutters, electrical tape, a voltmeter, and splice caps, then it would seem reasonable to assume that the person is an electrician. When you look at the tools that God has placed in the spiritual tool belt of your life, then you can think of them as indicators of what God wants you to use to accomplish your life's purpose.

So if you are someone who has the spiritual gifts of mercy, faith, and helping, you may be a natural person to focus on caring for the physical and spiritual well-being of others. If, on the other hand, you have the gifts of wisdom, leadership, and evangelism, you may be called to be a church planter. Gifts are not determinative; they do not limit us to certain careers or positions in ministry. However, they are the tools we can use to engage in our ministry the best we can.

There are a number of biblical passages that serve as the grounding for the principle of spiritual gifts. The best known comes from 1 Corinthians 12. In this passage, Paul is addressing a problem in the church of Corinth. The members have become highly competitive with each other and argue that various gifts and abilities serve as a ranking for who God loves more and who God loves less. Paul invokes the image of the human body and of how it only functions well when all of the various parts work together in harmony. Though the organs are different from one another, they are not ranked in order of importance; they are all needed. Paul compares this to the church. Each of us serves a different function, but our distinctions do not mean that some are more important than others. For the church to be vibrant and healthy, everyone needs to be using his spiritual gifts in harmony. Just as it makes no sense for the eye to tell the hand that it is no longer needed, it also makes no sense for someone with the gift of leadership to tell someone with the gift of mercy that she is unnecessary in the church.

In Romans 12, Paul again uses the image of the body as an analogy for the church, and he adds a call that it is essential for us to use our gifts in the church. In verses 4–8, we read:

> For just as each of us has one body with many members, and these members do not all have the same function, so in Christ we, though many, form one body, and each member belongs to all the others. We have different gifts, according to the grace given to each of us. If your gift is prophesying, then prophesy in accordance with your faith; if it is serving, then serve; if it is teaching, then teach; if it is to encourage, then give encouragement; if it is giving, then give generously; if it is to lead, do it diligently; if it is to show mercy, do it cheerfully.

In Ephesians 4, he reminds his readers of why this all is so important. In verses 12–13, he explains that in using our gifts, we "equip [Christ's] people for works of service, so that the body of Christ may be built up until we all reach unity in the faith and in the knowledge of the Son of God and become mature, attaining to the whole measure of the fullness of Christ." The key to this is understanding that it is not a matter of an individual doing what she or he thinks is best and the church benefiting from that contribution. This is an attitude that is more steeped in the contemporary cult of individualism than in anything that Christianity teaches. Instead, what Paul is talking about here is the principle that it is in our work with others, not just for others, that the body of Christ is built up.

We each play an important and unique part, but the body is only built when all of the unique parts come together for the glory of God. This concept may be counterintuitive in today's society, but it shows why it is so essential for the faith to be lived in the context of community and why the church is something that Jesus established himself before returning to heaven. And, in a provocative thing for Protestants to consider, it should be remembered that Jesus did not give us the Bible, he gave us the church. The Bible came three hundred years later and was finalized and accepted as the canon in the context of a meeting of church bishops. In theological systems where the Bible is seen as everything and the church as a mere inconvenience, this fact may be worth reconsidering! However, this may be a topic best left for a different occasion to explore.

Another important principle on the subject of spiritual gifts is that people do not get to choose their gifts. A gift is not something you have because you have decided you want it; it is not something you have because you have decided to develop it; and it is certainly not something you have because you agreed to serve on a specific committee in a church! I have seen countless examples of someone agreeing to serve on a committee who almost immediately begins to behave as though he has specific subject matter expertise! Gifts are given to us by God through the Holy Spirit. Gifts are given to us in accordance with what

God has decided our life's purpose is going to be. We may go through much of our life without ever knowing our gifts are present, and we can work on developing our gifts, but that does not mean we add or remove them. Gifts come from God, and from God alone. Gifts must also be seen in the context of being the tools to accomplish our life's purpose. They are not an end in themselves; they are the means to an end.

For example, I cannot decide that I want the gift of teaching regardless of how much I may want to be a teacher. However, if I do have the gift, I can still develop it by studying how to teach, exploring educational theory, and working at public speaking. An area of confusion for some people is that even though they do not possess a spiritual gift, they find themselves working in an area associated with one. For example, some people who teach may be very surprised to discover that they do not have the spiritual gift of teaching. Does this mean that they should immediately stop teaching? That depends on a number of factors, but their lack of gifting does mean that they will be unlikely to find the same fulfillment, joy, and energy from teaching that they would find in other areas that are more directly connected to their spiritual gifts. In my own life, I found that I do not have the gift of administration. However, I have sat in countless committee meetings in church and on the boards of directors of several nonprofit organizations. I have at times enjoyed the work (really!) and have learned much from doing it, but it has seldom given me the emotional charge or sense of excitement that working in my areas of giftedness does. The point is that we can work in a variety of ways that are outside our giftedness, but it is important to know our gifts and engage in significant work in our areas of giftedness because this is where we will be at our best and at our happiest.

There are a number of spiritual gifts discernment courses on the market today. The best one I have encountered is called *What You Do Best in the Body of Christ* by Bruce Bugbee. This course actually has three goals. It helps students to identify their core passion in life, their style (structured or unstructured, and people- or task-driven), and their spiritual gifts. The spiritual gifts section includes a survey with 137 specific statements that are rated and then self-scored by the participant. At the end of the survey, the participants will see that they have anywhere from 2 to 5 specific spiritual gifts, out of a possible 23, that work in a way that is much stronger than other gifts. There are a number of courses available to help individuals and groups to identify their spiritual gifts and some use highly sophisticated diagnostic tools to help assess them. Seek out one that you can take.

Name the spiritual gifts class you will be taking and when you will take it:

_____

_____

_____

_____

Why Do You Love Jesus?

Too many Westerners have a cerebral understanding of Jesus. We can "surrender our lives to Christ" and then go about our lives as if nothing has changed just because we have made a "decision."

We make the mistake of thinking that by merely agreeing about who Jesus is, everything is all set. Too many theological debates only seek agreement on ideas or principles and leave people to draw the erroneous conclusion that the goal is just to get agreement on specific issues. Of course, intellectual assent to doctrinal truth is essential, but it is not the end of the story.

If we are to be in a relationship, we need to be able to name the important characteristics of that relationship. We need to name the theological reasons for loving Jesus (the significance of the Incarnation, the power of the Atonement, etc.), but we need to name the relational reasons as well. Do you long to spend time with him in prayer? Do you seek his guidance on little things in daily life and not just in the big things? Do you feel like you have an "off" day if you do not spend time in prayer? Can you name how your relationship has deepened over the past six months, or is it something that isn't growing and maturing at a clear pace?

When academics use the term Christology, they are talking about their understanding of who Jesus is. When God is described as Trinity (Father, Son, and Holy Ghost), this means that God has come to earth as Jesus to make the relationship with humanity concrete. No longer can God be seen as distant or removed from human struggles. Jesus laughed, Jesus cried, Jesus became angry, and Jesus was tempted to sin. In the life of Jesus, God physically experienced all that each person experiences—and God suffered in ways that go far beyond anything any of us has ever suffered. Most profoundly, God did it all out of love, a love that each of us needs to live up to in our own lives. Certainly, it is essential for Christians to have a deep sense of gratitude and thankfulness for grace, but that is different from love. I am thankful to George Washington for being the father of my county, but I do not love him in a personal way. I am thankful to the university where I earned a doctorate, but I do not love it in a personal way. I need to be thankful to Jesus for the sacrifice he made that earned me a trip to heaven, but that is not enough! Jesus calls for us to love him in a very personal way and to be in a personal relationship with him. Many Christians argue that they do love and have a relationship with Jesus, but when pushed a little, they reveal that their feelings are actually feelings of gratitude and an intellectual sense of respect. This is different from a loving relationship!

Being able to name why you love Jesus is an important exercise, because it helps to show the state of your spiritual development. It shows if yours is merely an intellectual understanding, or if it is one rooted in the emotions and experiences of any loving relationship. Actually, it is a healthy exercise to be able to name why you love your spouse. Much is said and learned by being able to (or not being able to) name specific reasons for why you love your spouse. The same can be said for your relationship with Jesus.

Name why you love Jesus:

What Are You Most Committed To?

I once heard a preacher say that it is quite easy to determine what your biggest priorities in life are. He could tell you what they are by looking at two things you own: your date book and your checkbook. This is one of those gut-wrenching statements we sometimes hear in sermons because it leaves little room for argument. If most of your money is spent on buying the latest fashions, then it forces you to admit you are materialistic. If most of your free time is spent away from home with friends, then you cannot honestly say your children are your biggest commitment. Where your treasure is, there your heart is—and there your checkbook and date book are also!

Once again, this is a question that does not ask what you should be committed to, or ask what you think you should be most committed to. It asks an honest question that shows where the priorities in your daily life actually lie. So, if you do not lie in bed at night worrying about whales, then do not say that saving the whales is a priority! If you do not work hard to eat well and exercise daily, then do not say you are most committed to physical health. If God plays little or no part in your daily life, then do not say that God is most important in your life!

So, what are you most committed to? What gets you the most excited to think about and to talk about? Is it your work? Do you sacrifice everything and everyone for the sake of your career? Are you most committed to a hobby? Is your hobby the first thing on your mind in the morning and the last thing on your mind as you go to sleep at night? Is it your family? Is every moment of the day spent thinking about them and planning for them?

Perhaps a good question to ask is, which area of your life are you always willing to sacrifice other areas for? Are you always willing to let a work project take you away from family commitments? Does the schedule of your children's activities automatically cancel every other activity and commitment you make? Spend time with your checkbook and with your date book and make an honest assessment of where your focus is, and then name to yourself what is most important. Being able to answer this question can offer rich insights! Of course, once you do this, it is also important to then be able to name what you *want* to be most committed to in your life.

Name what you want to be most committed to in your life, and list at least three action steps you will take immediately to transition to these:

Who Needs Your Love the Most?

We do not live our lives in a vacuum. Community is essential for Christians. There is much that we need to do for our own growth, but we are also called to care for others. This is why Jesus left us the church when he returned to heaven. In Genesis, after Cain killed his brother Abel, God came to Cain and asked him where his brother was. Cain's response was that famous statement, "Am I my brother's keeper?" (Gen. 4:9). Of course, the implication was that the answer would be "no." But, in truth, the answer is "yes." We each are called to be our brother's keeper. We each are called to care for one another, to support one another, to grow in faith with one another, and to know how each other is doing.

Each of us should be able to name who relies on us and who needs our love the most in our lives. Perhaps these questions can help. Whose life is better because you are involved in it? Whose life would be most affected if you were no longer in it? Whose growth is best helped by your love? To whom do you feel most responsible and about whom would you feel the worst if you let them down? Why?

Once you are able to name who needs your love the most, it may be helpful to spend some time thinking about why they do, how you fulfill their need for your love, and how this relationship affects you and your own growth as a Christian. It is common to put our love in one place, and our time and energy someplace else. They need to be together; otherwise, our heart is living a lie.

Name who needs your love the most:

Conclusion

Take some time to look over the differences between how you answered the questions in Chapter Two versus how you have answered the questions in this chapter. The difference marks the work that you have established for yourself in developing a Rule for Life. Sometimes there are disproportionately large gaps between the two. Let this be an exciting description of who God is uniquely calling you to be, and let it be a clarion call to how your worldview should be shaped.

In the midst of this work, it is both helpful and important to remember that God's love is not forced upon us. It is offered to us and we must accept it in order to feel its full benefit. God will break through our darkness and through our stubbornness at times, but this breaking through comes only to the degree that we can accept it. This means that the issue is more about how far we are willing to let God in than about how far God is willing to come. This distinction is important because it centers on the gift of free will that each of us have been given. If God violates our free will, then we lose our ability to offer true love in return.

Now that we have gone through the work of defining both who we are and who we understand God is calling us to be, it is time to move on to the next step, which is to spell out specific spiritual disciplines that we will engage in to help define, build, and fulfill the life that God intended for us to live.

6

How to Develop a Rule for Life, Part II
Developing Your Disciplines

"The purpose of the Disciplines is liberation from the stifling slavery of self-interest and fear."

—**Richard Foster,** *Celebration of Discipline*

In Matthew 25, Jesus tells the parable of the talents as one of several ways to describe the kingdom of heaven. This powerful story offers an important lesson about working diligently. In the first century, a "talent" was an enormous unit of currency. In fact, it was estimated that the average laborer would have to work for twenty years in order to earn a single talent! So, if the average American today earns fifty thousand dollars per year, a single talent would be the equivalent of a million dollars and five talents would be worth five million dollars. That is a lot of money! In the story, Jesus explains that a man was going on a journey, so he entrusted one of his servants with five talents, another with two talents, and a third with one talent. While gone, the first two servants went out and doubled their money! The third buried his in the ground to keep it safe. Upon his return, the man commended the servants who doubled their money and condemned the third. In fact, the line used to commend the first two is the one most Christians hope to hear from God at the moment of their death: "Well done, good and faithful servant . . . enter into the joy of your lord" (NKJV).

Have you ever wondered how this situation could happen? What options are there to double someone's money in the span of time it would take for them to go on a trip? Would investing in bank CDs do it? How about investing in safe municipal bonds? No way! The only way to double your money in a relatively short period of time is to aggressively invest in something risky! A hot stock tip might do this; winning the lottery could do it as well. But there isn't much more!

So how is this an example of the kingdom of heaven? It is a lesson in not being complacent. It teaches us that God has entrusted each of us with some very valuable gifts and abilities, and he expects us to use them aggressively for the kingdom. If we do not, and allow them to hide in a hole, then God isn't going to be very happy with us. This chapter is about using those gifts in a structured and meaningful way.

In his classic text, *Celebration of Discipline: The Path to Spiritual Growth*, Richard Foster shows how spiritual disciplines are anything but boring, tedious, and suffocating. In fact, he writes:

> Joy is the keynote of all the Disciplines. The purpose of the Disciplines is liberation from the stifling slavery to

self-interest and fear. When the inner spirit is liberated from all that weighs it down, it can hardly be described as dull drudgery. Singing, dancing, even shouting characterize the Disciplines of the spiritual life. (2)

This may seem counterintuitive. How can anything with the word "discipline" in the title be a source of joy? The key is in remembering that the goal of disciplines is to help us return to the relationship and life that God intended from the beginning of time. In becoming who we were intended to be all along, we find peace and joy. However, this journey into wholeness does not happen accidentally. If we are serious about developing spiritually, given all of the challenges we face, then it is very important to have a set of disciplines to practice.

This is a principle that makes a lot of sense in other areas of life. If you seek to lose weight, you need a set of disciplines in order to do so effectively. You might cut out snacks, exercise daily, eat healthier food, and stop drinking soda. Each of these steps contributes to an effective diet, but how many of these to take on and the degree of dedication to them will vary widely from person to person. There is no single formula for the best diet.

If you seek to improve your level of physical fitness, you also need an effective set of disciplines. The kinds of exercise you're interested in, the pace that is appropriate for your age and body type, the equipment needed, and the perseverance to maintain the discipline over time—all these contribute to a description of fitness. The mix of disciplines will again vary by individual, but they all serve the same purpose. There is room for personal preference, personal tastes, and experimentation and adventure, but the goal of improved fitness is the same.

If you seek to learn a language, you need a discipline of time spent studying vocabulary, of reading and speaking the language. If you seek to become well-read in a particular subject, you need a discipline of learning about which sources provide the best information, of reading about the subject, of talking with others about the subject, and of continuing to learn about the subject. These are just a few of the endless examples of how any significant goal requires a set of disciplines and practice to achieve it.

Listed below are a series of spiritual disciplines that can contribute to spiritual growth. Variation will occur in how individuals select and incorporate each discipline into their lives. Additionally, as you grow, the mix of disciplines will change to suit where you are in each stage of the journey. The particular mix of disciplines is not nearly as important as establishing and maintaining a specific Rule for Life over time, especially when challenging, painful, or stressful times in life arise.

M. Basil Pennington, in his writings about spiritual growth, talks about how Cistercian (Trappist) monks believe that repetition is the mother of wisdom. It is in repeating the disciplines, the prayers, and the reading of Scripture over long periods of time that deeper meanings are revealed, deeper understanding comes, and deeper love grows. They do not believe in being spiritual dilettantes where people flit about from one practice to another as their attention span, or lack thereof, dictates. They instead plumb the depths of meaning found in a single set of disciplines. The analogy can be made to the digging of a well. Water is not found by digging a little bit in dozens of different holes, but by persistently digging in a single hole. The view may get boring, but you are more likely to reach the depths to find water. Cistercians see that the same is true spiritually. By digging deeper within the context of a set of disciplines, one is more likely to reach the living water.

Daily Prayer Discipline

Prayer is the foundational discipline of the spiritual life. It is around prayer that everything else is built. Like Benedict's Rule for his monks, prayer is the center of daily life, and everything else fits around it. St. Padre Pio is credited with saying, "Prayer is oxygen for the soul." Prayer is the very essence of our relationship with God because it is where the relationship is nurtured and developed. Just as breathing nourishes and feeds our bodies with oxygen, prayer nourishes and feeds our souls.

There are different kinds of prayer. We can praise God for the grandness of who he is; we can cry out to him in distress when we are in trouble; we can bring a question or a concern to God; and we can sit quietly and listen to God speak with us. One classic explanation of prayer used the acronym A.C.T.S. to describe four different types of prayer: "A" stands for adoration. This is when we praise God for who God is. We celebrate God's glory, God's goodness, God's majesty, and God's sovereignty. "C" stands for confession. A very important form of prayer is to confess our sins to God and to seek forgiveness. When sins go unconfessed, they fester and serve as a corrosive force on our souls. "T" stands for thanksgiving. Prayers of thanksgiving are very important because they show not only gratitude, but also help ensure that we never take God's blessings for granted. "S" stands for supplication. These are the prayers where we ask God to intercede in the problems we or those around us face.

Another method of prayer that is common in Roman Catholic, Anglican, and Orthodox circles is to pray the Daily Office. The Daily Office is a modification of the monastic cycle of daily prayer and allows individuals to engage in much the same kind of prayer they do. At minimum, the Daily Office includes a set of morning and evening prayers, but there are usually afternoon and night prayers as well. Typically, praying the Daily Office revolves around a recitation of the Book of Psalms (The Roman Catholic *Liturgy of the Hours* rotates through all of the Psalms every four weeks, and the *Anglican Book of Common Prayer* goes through them every six weeks). Added to the Psalms is a set of other readings from Scripture and intercessory prayers for oneself, as well as for others. A key feature of the Daily Office is that it keeps our prayer from becoming little more than a litany of requests of what we want from God. The use of so much Scripture keeps the focus on God and not on us. It also helps us remember that we belong to a wider church, and the church needs prayer as well. People who regularly pray the Daily Office often say that it provides the structure and framework within which they live their daily lives.

Each of the kinds of prayer described above represents a prayer where we do the speaking and God does the listening. This is the first part of an effective prayer life. The next part of an effective prayer life centers on listening. One method of prayer that has a long history in Christian monasteries and has been more generally popular in recent decades is centering prayer. This form of prayer is a meditative exercise that takes time to develop. In centering prayer, the goal is to spend twenty minutes (or more) at a time sitting in God's presence and saying nothing, just listening. A word or phrase is used as the "center" to keep distractions from entering into the mind. For example, if one were to use the "Jesus Prayer" as the center, you would sit, relax, close your eyes, and each time you breathe out, you would say to yourself "Lord Jesus Christ, have mercy on me, a sinner." The specific center word or phrase is not as important as the fact that we use it well. Some of the more common centering terms are: Jesus, Adonai, Christ, love, peace, and I love you, Lord. Whatever center you choose, you would say it slowly and quietly with each exhalation. After you have become relaxed, you would stop repeating the centering phrase and would just sit in God's presence. When a distraction or random thought enters your mind, you do not focus on it, or even get frustrated that it is there. You just wait for the next exhalation, return to the centering phrase, and repeat it with each exhalation until the distraction is gone. Given the frenetic pace of contemporary life, many beginners in centering prayer become easily frustrated because their minds contain a constant stream of distracting thoughts. Do not let this discourage you! In time (often measured in weeks and months rather than days), the mind learns how to let go of these distractions and focus more and more on God.

A beginner will be lucky to be able to spend five minutes in centering prayer. A good goal would be to reach the point where you spend twenty minutes twice a day praying this way. The key to developing an ability to do centering prayer is consistency. This is a practice that does not come quickly or easily, but it is a powerful one because it teaches you to listen and to feel the presence of God in a manner you might not otherwise experience. To learn it properly requires perseverance. However, remember that the goal of centering prayer is not to draw closer to God, which is not possible because God is always close! The goal is to sense God's closeness more clearly. It is also important not to set goals, establish expectations, or try to control the process. It is important to come before God as an empty vessel for God to fill as he sees fit.

Basil Pennington has defined three rules (or guides) for centering prayer. They are:

1. Remember that God is at the very center of your being.
2. Use your centering word or phrase and let it help remove all other distractions.
3. Whenever you become aware of anything, return to the centering word until it passes. (54)

There is a tradition from the church fathers that states, "So long as a man is aware he is praying, he is not yet praying" (Pennington 76). Even the awareness that you are praying must be left behind in centering prayer.

This is different from the kind of meditation practiced by Buddhists and Hindus. In Eastern religions, the goal of meditation is to try to completely empty the mind and to stay there. Reality is seen as an illusion, so the goal in meditation is to remove oneself from reality as much as possible. The goal is to achieve emptiness and nothingness. This is very different from centering prayer! In Christian meditation, the goal is to clear the mind of distractions so one can focus entirely on God. It is not a process of emptying and experiencing nothingness; it is instead a process of clearing out distractions so that one can be fully in the presence of God.

It should also be noted that centering prayer has many side benefits. Practitioners of the method develop a strong sense of inner calm and serenity, and they often experience better health due to lower levels of stress. These benefits are all true and wonderful, but they are not the most significant reasons for centering prayer. The goal is not to feel more calm; the goal is more God! Enjoy the benefits, but do not focus on them—focus on the glory of feeling the closeness of God and on being able to better hear God's call on your life and for your life!

As time passes, the ultimate goal is neither to focus on speaking or listening. The goal is to be able to just be in God's presence. Much like a married couple whose love has grown over many years and who have reached the point where just being in each other's company is an experience of bliss, a Christian with many years of prayer gradually learns to experience the quiet bliss of just being in God's presence. There are other types of prayer in addition to those just described. The key is to develop a healthy and disciplined prayer life that listens to God in a meaningful way.

The centrality of prayer among the spiritual disciplines cannot be overstated. Without a solid grounding in prayer, a person cannot properly develop the other disciplines. A healthy spiritual life and a meaningful Rule for Life develop from the center of prayer. Without prayer, we risk going off very quickly on any of a number of oddly self-indulgent tangents.

Describe the prayer discipline you will commit to:

_____

_____

_____

_____

Discipline of Bible Study

The Bible is sometimes called the owner's manual for the Christian soul. The Bible is the narrative of the faith we fit in to. It is not a cookbook formula for what we are to do and not to do in life (that would be too easy!). Instead, it is the narrative of the history of God's relationship with humanity. It shows the intended nature of creation, how humanity broke the relationship, and how God has worked through history to restore the relationship. It also shows how the story is going to end.

It is an all-too-common practice for people who are newly excited about the faith to decide that they will read the entire Bible cover to cover. They get through the amazing stories of Genesis and of how Moses led the Hebrews out of slavery in Egypt in the book of Exodus, but they then get lost in the details of Leviticus and Deuteronomy. The seemingly endless listing of dietary and behavioral laws kills their interest in the Bible faster than a dull sermon loses the attention of its hearers! Reading the Bible cover to cover can be an important experience in one's piety, but it may not be the best way to begin to learn seriously about the faith.

Given the sweep of history, the times and places that are so foreign to us that they seem barely comprehensible, and the complex weave of the narrative that flows through all of Scripture, the best way to approach a serious study of the Bible is as part of a formal Bible study group. Studying the Bible with others is also a good way to protect oneself from coming to inaccurate conclusions and then making life decisions based on the inaccurate reading of the texts. This has happened far too often, and it has often had disastrous consequences.

In undertaking a formal study of the Bible, you learn of the economic, historic, political, military, and spiritual dynamics that are at work in the stories you are reading. You not only come to better appreciate what incredible leaders David and Solomon were, but you also learn about how flawed and human they really were. You learn about how different the time of Isaiah was when he saw the northern kingdom of Israel destroyed by the Assyrians in 722 BC from that of Jeremiah when he saw the southern kingdom of Judah destroyed by the Babylonians in 586 BC. You learn of the struggles of Elijah and of the hardships of Haggai and of how they both stayed faithful to God no matter what. Most importantly, you learn of the repeated faithlessness of humanity and of God's promise to offer forgiveness and redemption to the world.

In the New Testament, we learn of the struggles of Israel living under the occupation of the Roman Empire and how Jesus repeatedly challenged the conventional wisdom of how one is to follow God. We learn why there was jurisdictional confusion over how to deal with Jesus after his arrest (involving the Sanhedrin of Jerusalem, the Roman governor Pontius Pilate, and King Herod of Galilee), and what all the symbolism of Holy Week means (palms, the sacrificial lamb, the bread, the wise, foot washing, the cross, and the empty tomb). We also learn how the church developed in the early years after the first Easter, and how Paul took the message of the gospel to the whole eastern half of the Roman Empire. Clarity on these matters helps to bring so much clarity to the faith!

Formal Bible study is different from a devotional study. Devotional studies are meant to serve as encouragement in the midst of daily struggles and are not focused on the more academic goals of the formal studies. Devotional studies are often best accompanied by devotional books. Daily devotionals have been popular for centuries, as have devotional guides that tend to draw attention to Bible passages that focus on specific challenges people face in life. In a typical daily devotional, there is an encouraging passage from Scripture, an inspirational story or message, and then a short prayer. The goal is to read the devotional in the morning and then think about it repeatedly as you go through the challenges of the day. There are classics like *My Utmost for His Highest* and the serial publication *Our Daily Bread*.

If possible, the best way to grapple with Scripture is to both be a part of a formal study group and to use a personal devotional as part of daily prayer.

Describe the Bible study regimen or regimens you will commit to:

Small Group Commitment

Throughout all of Christian history, people have gathered in smaller groups within the church for prayer, support, study, and nurture. The word "disciple" in the singular appears 28 times in the New Testament in the NIV Bible. The plural form, disciples, appears 266 times (Dean 176). We are meant to learn and grow together. Given the culture of the early twenty-first century, this can be challenging because we are more accustomed to being alone and to keeping our faith life a personal matter. To find the words to express what we are experiencing and to share with others (especially people we are not even sure we like) is a daunting task! However, by being in a group, we get to practice sharing love with others, we learn how to be in relationship with people who are different from us, we have the opportunity to offer support to others when they are in need, and we learn how to accept support from others when we need it.

This is all stuff that cannot be learned in a book. Relationships are messy, stressful, frustrating, and even disappointing. They also take a long time to develop and nurture. Learning to deal with all of this can only take place when we live our faith with others. This is how we learn to "love our neighbors as ourselves" (see Mark 12:31).

Describe your commitment to a small group:

_____

_____

_____

_____

Who Are You Actively Praying For?

A problem that sometimes arises in prayer is that we come to the inaccurate conclusion that prayer is just something that happens between God and us. Though this is an essential part of prayer, it is not all of prayer. We must remember the needs of others when we pray. We go before God not just on our own behalf, but on behalf of others as well. This helps remind us that ours is not a solitary journey. It is the timeless journey of the church that individuals have the amazing opportunity to participate in. So if our individual prayer lives are to be healthy, they need to include prayers for others and not just for ourselves. Therefore, it is important to be able to state who we are praying for.

Who are you praying for to receive salvation? Given the culture of today, more people are living and suffering while they are estranged from God. It is heartbreaking to think that people we know and care for may spend an eternity estranged from God because they were unable to find God in this life. For those of us who have found God, this creates a significant responsibility to help these people who are lost. The Great Commission of Matthew 28 calls all Christians to work to help "make disciples of all nations." This means that we should be thinking about people we know and are close to who do not have a meaningful relationship with God. The first step in helping them to find God is to pray for them regularly. We need to pray that God will soften their hearts, that they will be more mindful of the presence of God in their lives, and that God will use each of us to help them find faith. For some people, the process of conversion comes quickly; for others, there can be years of continuous prayer before something spiritually significant happens. The key is, we must be able to name who we are praying for to find God and to continually pray for them, regardless of the results over time.

Who are you praying for to receive God's healing touch? Because of the amount of suffering and pain in this world, it is fairly safe to say that each of us knows quite a few people who need healing in one form or another in their lives. They need to know that God cares for them in their time of struggle and they need to know that God's people care for them as well. Asking someone if there is anything you can pray about on their behalf can become a profoundly holy moment. Even people with profound spiritual lives face difficulties and trials. Praying on their behalf is both effective and important in the life Christians share together. I personally remember an experience when our church was going through a particularly difficult time, and for months I could feel the power of the prayer that others were offering to God on my behalf. Words cannot describe the power, but I felt it all in the very depths of my soul. I did not have the strength to get through the challenges of those days on my own. It was the active prayers of intercession of others on my behalf that made the difference and provided me with strength. Prayer is that powerful!

Who are you praying for to experience growth? The question of salvation is one of life and death. The question of growth is one of whether we are experiencing the full meaning of life. We are all called to grow. In his poem "Cleon," the great British poet Robert Browning wrote, "Why stay we on the earth unless to grow?" Without growth there is little meaning to life. In prayer, we must not only focus on our own growth, but also on the growth of others around us. We can pray for others as they seek wisdom, perseverance, discernment, and serenity.

Who are you praying for to receive God's protection? Everyone faces dangers. Asking God to protect others is both an act of faith in God and an act of love for those we pray for. In my own prayer life, I daily ask God to give strength, guidance, and wisdom to my bishop, my pastor, and to the clergy and lay leaders of my church. I pray for them so that they can better lead me in the life of our church.

For whom are you praying, and what are you praying for in each case?

What Do You Do for Fun?

Does this seem like a strange question to ask in the midst of a discussion of spiritual disciplines? What does fun have to do with religion? Fun matters on two levels. First, it is good for the human body and soul. To always be serious or to always work is harmful for both physical and emotional health. Secondly, we are told in Genesis that after God spent six days creating the world, he rested on the seventh. Does God really need to rest? Of course not! However, God was modeling what he wants us to do because we do need rest.

For the people of the Old Testament, the Sabbath was a reminder that after the Exodus, they were no longer slaves, because slaves were never allowed a day off. The Sabbath reminded them of their freedom as well as of their salvation by God. Their use of the Sabbath as a day of rest, as a time for fun with the family, and for worship showed that they placed family and God as priorities over the work of the rest of the week. For people today, freedom from slavery may not be so compelling an image, but we may struggle with seeing ourselves as being more like machines than people. Well, Sabbath rest also reminds us that we are not machines, because machines are not allowed to take time off. We are precious children of God who deserve time to rest and to enjoy the beauty and blessings of God's creation. Sabbath is a built-in concept that calls people to take time to "smell the roses." In other words, it reminds us that not only are our lives a precious gift, but all of creation is a precious gift as well. Additionally, when we spend time in the midst of God's creation, we can praise God for the beauty of it all. We can do this on a mountain, on a lake, in admiring the majesty of a sunset, at the seashore enjoying time with loved ones, or in any other of a myriad of ways God has placed beauty in his creation. If we do not take time away from the daily routines of work, deadlines, appointments, and chores, then we are ignoring a truly precious gift that God offers. I have always been suspicious of clergy and of academics who do not laugh and have fun. By always being serious and formal, they do not experience the ravishing beauty and mirth of God's creation and the silly people he has filled it with!

Describe what you will do for fun:

_____

_____

_____

_____

What Do You Do for Your Family?

When St. Benedict looked for a model for his monasteries, he decided to model them on the family. He saw the intensity of relationship, the commitment, the loyalty, the shared responsibility, and the love as qualities that he wanted to emulate in the monasteries. Your family is made up of those people who are closest to you and who cannot so easily abandon you when times get tough. Is it a close and loving relationship, or is it one that has strains and fractures? Do you sacrifice for your family? Is spending time with family a priority? Can your family count on you? Do you rely on your family?

These are all questions that are meant to help explore the nature of relationship with family and to see if there are particular areas that need attention and effort. Families are seldom perfect (we all have a crazy relative or two . . . I can't be the only one!), so they provide plenty of opportunity to learn how to love, how to cherish, and how to model the virtues that the Christian faith calls us to live by.

Describe what you will do with your family:

What Do You Do for Your Church?

When churches function well, they can model the best qualities of a family. They exhibit love, sacrificial service, and a commitment to stay together through thick and thin. However, it seems that many churches have drifted into the trap of focusing on professionalism. They try to be like the business world and seek to hire trained clergy and professional lay specialists to lead the ministries. Pastors are earning doctor of ministry degrees in record numbers, Sunday school directors are earning masters degrees in education, and so on. We have the best educated professionals in the history of the church, yet in the West, the church is at a historic low point. The professionalization of the church staff has created the sense that the church can only function efficiently and well if all of the leaders are paid professionals who understand the latest theories and practices of their sub-specialties. Because of this, laity in many churches have scaled back their efforts at participation because they have a sense that they are unqualified to engage in meaningful ministry. Fortunately, many are now concluding that this direction is in fact harming the church because it is absolving everyone but the paid leadership of responsibility for ministry. A shift is now moving from looking to business models to organize church life and toward thinking in terms of family once again. Everyone needs to participate and serve in the life of the parish if it is to thrive. As the expression goes, everyone at some point needs to take off the bib and put on the apron. What is your relationship with your church? Are you wearing a bib and focusing on having the church feed you? Or have you put on the apron and begun to work to serve others?

Describe what you will do for your church:

How Do You Serve Your Community?

This may seem like an odd question. If it is important for us to get more involved and to serve in our churches, then how can we at the same time be thinking about how we can better serve our communities? The answer is simple, yet profoundly important. The primary reason people become Christians is because they see Christians living the kinds of lives and knowing the kind of peace they want for themselves. People in our postmodern world have chosen self-centered hedonism because they think it will bring happiness, and it is only a matter of time before they discover that it cannot. If they do not give up and sink into depression at this point, they will then look to other places and to other people to try and find happiness. Visibility in and commitment to the community is an important way that Christians offer our faith as an alternative to the lies of this world.

We have a powerful example of this from history. In the fifth century, St. Patrick went from community to community in Ireland and converted people with his life more than with his words. It wasn't that he gave a better sermon, was a better teacher, or that he used better illustrations in his message. Instead, it was the joy and the simplicity of his life that people found so compelling. Just a few minutes with Patrick showed people the power of the Christian faith and how it brings answers to all of life's problems. People wanted to be Christians themselves because they wanted what Patrick had. In the thirteenth century, St. Francis of Assisi was using a similar approach and is often credited with the sentiment, "Preach the Gospel every day, and if you have to, use words." He argued that how we act and how we live says more to others about our faith than the words we choose to say. So, how do you preach the gospel to your community?

Describe how you are serving your community:

_____

_____

_____

_____

What Sacrifices Are You Currently Making?

The Christian life is a life of sacrifice. There is always more that needs to be done than we can do and there are always more people to help than we can help. So, we should be working up at least a bit of a sweat in following the path God calls us to! We should recognize the severity of the need and have a sense of urgency about meeting that need. This is what Jesus meant when he said, "The harvest is plentiful, but the workers are few" (Luke 10:2a).

Additionally, it is important to understand that what we have does not really belong to us. We are called to be stewards of what actually belongs to God. To be a steward is to be a caretaker of property belonging to another. At many churches, the prayer offered when the collection is taken each week is, "All things come of thee, and of thine own have we given thee," which is a direct quote from the King James Version of 1 Chronicles 29:14b. A healthy Christian worldview includes the understanding that God made everything and that we are caretakers of it, while we spend our few short years on earth. This does not allow for complacency or for laziness while others toil diligently at the work set before us.

Can you name the sacrifices you are making in your life right now because of your faith in Christ? What are you doing that you would not be doing if your life was not dedicated to Christ? Or, to put it in another way, what are you NOT doing right now that you would be doing if you were not devoted to God? There should be things that have been sacrificed for the gospel. If you cannot name anything, then does that say anything about the seriousness with which you are answering God's call?

Describe the sacrifices you are making for your faith:

What Weaknesses Are You Working On?

We all have weaknesses. An important part of intentionally working toward growth is the ability to name our weaknesses. Weaknesses come in all shapes and sizes and hit people in different ways. What may be a non-issue for one person can be an enormous burden for another. It is very hard to know how to address these weaknesses and to work on them if we cannot first name them. So, what are a few of your weaknesses? Do you struggle with an addiction? Do you struggle with behavioral problems? Are you struggling with relationship issues? Do you struggle with spending too much time in escapism? Do you have a lack of faith? Are you caught up in the rat race and the values of this culture? Are you so easily distracted that it negatively affects your career or relationships? Do you take advantage of friends and loved ones? Do you struggle with selfishness? Can others trust you? Can others rely on you? The list of questions could go on and on, but the point is that we need to be ruthlessly honest in this. We need to be able to name our weaknesses, and we need to make a commitment about what we will do in order to work through them. A disciplined practice of the Examination of Conscience (Examen) is going to be essential in being able to do this.

I have a friend who is a third generation alcoholic. He was well aware of the terrible damage that alcohol has done to his family for generations, but he felt there was little he could do to change the pattern because drinking was the only effective way he could deal with his struggles in life. After a near-fatal accident, he decided that his life and his children were worth fighting for. He entered Alcoholics Anonymous, developed a prayer life, became active in church, and got active in a fraternal organization in his community. He also learned about how to deal with addiction. He became dependent upon God, he got more active in the lives of his children, and he found ways to socialize with people that did not involve drinking. It was a long and hard journey, but with faith in God, hard work, being surrounded by people who loved him, and a willingness to press on despite setbacks, he lived a much happier and more meaningful life.

I have another friend who struggled with being a very negative and pessimistic person. Friendships have been lost over his constant whining, complaining, and insistence on seeing the bad in everything. He finally named this issue and made a commitment to live a life of joy instead of a life of negativity. He refused to say bad things, he forced himself to look for the positive in life experiences, and he concentrated on finding things to compliment in people. This was an enormously difficult struggle for him, and it took a long time before lasting change settled in. For a while, he had to stop himself from speaking every time he wanted to say something and remember his commitment to changing behavior. It took more than a year before he felt that he had changed enough to the point where he did not have to regulate his speech so much. He had regular slip-ups throughout this process, but they became fewer and farther between as he worked on changing his attitude about life. Eventually, not only did he change what he said, but he found that this exercise also changed how he felt. Slowly, he became a happier, more optimistic, and more generally positive individual, and this impacted his whole quality of life.

Describe the weaknesses you are working on:

_____

_____

_____

_____

Conclusion

This is not the kind of book that can be read and then put aside. At the same time, the set of exercises described above is not meant to be a cookbook-style recipe for success, nor are they things you need to adopt all at once. The process being described here is one that will take time and energy. Someone once asked St. Teresa of Avila about how to do contemplative prayer. Her response was "Say the Our Father, but take an hour to say it" (Pennington 115). So, my prayer for you is that you will be able to take days or even weeks with each of the questions above and learn what God is calling you to do.

These exercises are not meant to make us feel bad about ourselves. If all of the things described above are new to you, good! This is the perfect book for you! The exercises are also not meant to serve as an opportunity for us to judge others. We do not have the wisdom or power to do so, *thank God!* The best we can do is to be fruit inspectors for our own lives.

This list is meant to lead you through a series of reflections on the kinds of disciplines that Christians engage in to help their spiritual growth and development. Building a life of discipleship and service must be done with great intentionality, one piece at a time.

My hope is that this chapter will show you just how important it is to be deliberate about developing your disciplines. As I have said before, if we do not do this deliberately, we will be overwhelmed by the urgency of everyday crises, and the disciplines of spiritual development will remain little more than a pious goal. So write down your responses over time, develop your own set of disciplines, and commit to following them. Then, put on your helmet and enjoy the ride!

7

How to Develop a Rule for Life, Part III
Dreaming Your Goals

"'For I know the plans I have for you,' declares the LORD,
'plans to prosper you and not to harm you,
plans to give you hope and a future.
Then you will call on me and come and pray to me,
and I will listen to you.'"

—Jeremiah 29:11–12

I heard a story about a man visiting a construction site and wondering what was going on. He went to one worker and asked what he was doing, and the worker said, "I'm laying bricks." The man went to another worker and asked what he was doing, and that worker said, "I'm constructing a wall." He went to a third worker who responded with a wide smile and said, "I'm building a cathedral!" All three were at the same site and doing similar work, but their perspectives on what they were doing were very different!

How do you see what you are doing in your life? Is there a sense that you are just doing the task set before you without question or reflection on it? Are you able to see a bigger picture, and do you see yourself moving in a direction that will lead to a meaningful accomplishment? As the story above illustrates, our understanding of our work may be more of a reflection of how we see life than of anything related to the work itself. We may lose sight of the big things as we trudge through day-to-day living. How many cathedral builders never really see that they are doing something magnificent that will last for generations? The goal of this chapter is to help you think through your goals in life so that moving toward them can be a part of your Rule for Life.

I remember once paying a hospital visit to an elderly parishioner. As I walked in the room and asked her how she was doing, she replied, "Getting old really sucks!" I was floored because these were strong words from someone who was eighty-five! As we sat together, she told me that when she was little, she thought her job was to do well in school. After she got married, she thought her job was to be a good wife. When children began to arrive, she thought her job was to be a good mother. When they married and had children, she thought her job was to be a good grandmother. Now, sitting in a hospital with a pessimistic prognosis, she wondered if she had spent her whole life thinking about the need of the day instead of the bigger picture of what God had called her to. She wanted to take all she had learned and apply it before her health gave out.

I found this to be a particularly difficult visit because I found the standard answers to be inadequate. I could tell her that her family was the task that God had called her to, but it was clear that she was looking for the meta-narrative within which her family life would have fit. I could also have told her that because her children and grandchildren had all turned out well, she had lived a successful life, but it was clear that she was thinking beyond that. She couldn't find the specific words that day and neither could I, but looking back on it, I wonder if she had wanted her life to have a kingdom purpose, within which she could then have lived her daily life and raised her children. In the terms of the example above, she would have been happy to lay bricks, but wanted to do so knowing that she was building a cathedral. Her regret in life was that she had never really seen the cathedral.

The notion of a goal or destination is an essential one in the Christian pilgrimage. Not only are individuals on a pilgrimage to eventually reach heaven, but the worldwide church is on a pilgrimage that has a very specific destination, which is described in the Book of Revelation. In chapter 21, we read:

> Then I saw "a new heaven and a new earth," for the first heaven and the first earth had passed away, and there was no longer any sea. I saw the Holy City, the New Jerusalem, coming down out of heaven from God, prepared as a bride beautifully dressed for her husband. And I heard a loud voice from the throne saying, "Look! God's dwelling place is now among the people, and he will dwell with them. They will be his people, and God himself will be with them and be their God. 'He will wipe away every tear from their eyes. There will be no more death' or mourning or crying or pain, for the old order of things has passed away." (Rev. 21:1–4)

Despite what every one of the more than three thousand advertisements you will see each day this week tell you, you are not here on earth to enjoy life, to consume as much as you can, or to accumulate stuff. We are here to be in a devoted relationship with God and to fulfill the purpose God has put us on earth to complete. He is focused on the building of his kingdom and has decided to invite us to participate in the work. If we are to contribute to it in a meaningful way, we need to see the bigger picture of life and strive to accomplish it. Yes, we are each called to build a meaningful life, but more important than that, we are called to build our life in the context of the building of the kingdom.

This is an amazing honor! God certainly does not need us to accomplish this goal, because the kingdom will not be completed until the second coming of Christ. However, God invites us to participate in this most holy of tasks, building it. Our response to that invitation must be more than going about our daily lives doing whatever we did before we had faith and feeling good about ourselves because we cognitively agree with the principles of the Bible and have therefore "surrendered our lives to Christ." Our surrender must result in dramatic changes within us! If we believe that God created us and that humanity has fallen from the ideal relationship with God, then our natural state is to be in that broken relationship! To merely say that we want to be in a restored relationship does not automatically lead to one. This is like saying that we are on a diet, but have made no changes in what we eat! If after we commit to becoming Christians, we continue to live our lives in the same way we lived them before, are we really on the Christian pilgrimage? If we believe we were made ON purpose, then it also means that we were made FOR a purpose. If we believe that we are to become more Christlike in our lives, then we must live our lives in a manner that actually does become more Christlike over time.

In other words, to be on pilgrimage does not mean that we get to sit at a bar, have a drink, and conclude that we are doing a great job just because we are that good of a person. To be on pilgrimage is to take a journey where we have experiences, meet challenges, learn lessons, and achieve a goal. For Christians, this goal is the experience of being in heaven for eternity, but because God invites us to participate in building the kingdom, our time on earth needs to be spent preparing our own lives for the work and then engaging in that work in a meaningful way.

The catch in all of this is that purposes differ for each person. We are not all called to do the same thing or to play the same role. One of the great challenges of the Christian life is for each Christian to find the purpose that God has created them to fulfill and to commit to that work. There are as many tasks in building the kingdom as there are people! We need to reach out, teach, help, support, serve, lead, care and pray for, and give to others. There may be times when each of us is called to do each of these things, but each of us will tend to focus on a few particular things God has wired us to do. Things we are not wired for tend to be hard, draining, and frustrating. Things we are wired for tend to be fun, exciting, and invigorating, because in doing them we are doing the very things we were created to do!

We do want to be careful, however, because there are dangers. One of the extreme dangers we face is to fall into the trap of thinking that there is some sort of "hierarchy of purpose." We see this illusion when someone thinks that they are somehow a better Christian than someone else is because they have a more important purpose. That idea is insane! Yet even in 1 Corinthians 3, Paul addresses this exact same issue in the earliest years of the church. At the time in Corinth, there was an argument among the people that basically claimed that your relative greatness as a Christian was determined by the greatness of the person who baptized you. In our day, it is easy to see the silliness in that notion, but we somehow cannot see that someone working in the church kitchen is no more or less loved by God than the person preaching the sermon to large crowds. This problem appears every time someone says, "Well, I'm just a lay person," or "I'm just a member of the ministry team." No one is "just" anything! There are many things we say and do that reveal the indwelling of this bias toward some ministry tasks and away from others. So, without fully understanding or realizing why, we create hierarchies in our heads and allow them to govern how we view the life of our church.

In Chapter Four, I cited Brother Lawrence, a poor and uneducated monk in seventeenth-century Paris. Because of his lack of education, he was tasked with working in the monastery kitchen. He spent the rest of his long life either working in the kitchen or repairing the sandals of the other monks. He never saw his work as menial or less important than that of others. For him, scrubbing a pot or sweeping a floor was as holy a moment as venerating the Sacrament on his knees. Because of this, every moment was a moment spent with God and every task was a task done for God. This approach to life and work so impressed the other monks around him that they were the ones who collected his sayings into the book called *The Practice of the Presence of God*, still wildly popular and in print today.

Brother Lawrence proved that there is no hierarchy in the tasks to be done in service to God. Instead, he showed, there does not even need to be a separation between the sacred and the secular. Every moment of every day could be spent with God, and every task could take on a holy function if done with the proper devotion to God.

Another danger is to draw the mistaken conclusion that God is calling each of us to do some amazing thing. Because of this, too many people jockey for positions of leadership and power believing that the only meaningful Christian life is the one where extraordinary things are taking place. This is a dangerous lie, and it is most commonly manifested in the idea that people need continual "mountaintop experiences" in their spiritual lives in order to remember that God is with them. Mountaintop experiences are wonderful, but we cannot control them, regulate them, or initiate them. This is work left to God. So, if we continually look for them, we are bound to be unnecessarily disappointed because they will not come when we want or desire them. The real work of the spiritual life is done in the midst of daily living. Remember, the intensity of Mt. Sinai lasted for only a short time, and it was followed by forty years of wandering in the wilderness as the people learned to obey God.

This may sound straightforward, but it is not. God does not call all of us to do extraordinary things. God calls us to do the ordinary things but to do them in an extraordinary manner. This was a painful lesson learned by Phil Vischer, the creator of VeggieTales. In 1993, he founded Big Idea Productions with Mike Nawrocki to produce video Bible stories for children. They were wildly successful and expanded to include books, toys, and games. Years later, Vischer would say in a *Christianity Today* interview that he had desperately wanted to be a Christian Walt Disney (Smietana). He wanted to expand Big Idea into a multimedia conglomerate that would offer faith-based resources in a variety of formats. It was in keeping with this vision that Big Idea produced *Jonah: A VeggieTales Movie*, in 2002. It met with some commercial success, but Vischer had stretched the company so far that he bankrupted it in the process and had to sell it to a secular media corporation. The short Bible story videos are still produced, but Vischer lost the company. In his *Christianity Today* interview, he said that the most important lesson he learned in the whole experience was that God had not created him to be a Christian Walt Disney. God had created him to be a Christian Phil Vischer. The best way to have done that would have been to discern and follow God's call and not his own desires. This same lesson applies to all of us. God does not want you to be like a famous or successful person in your field—he created you to be you.

When we tire of our roles and responsibilities, it helps to remember God has planted us in a certain place and told us to be a good accountant or teacher or mother or father. Christ expects us to be faithful where he puts us, and when he returns, we will be invited to rule together with him. These are words that most Christians hear over the years, but when you stop and think about the reality, it is mind-blowing. We spend our lives trying to be God and failing, yet when we surrender control of our lives to Jesus and live as he calls us to, we are invited by God to help lead all of creation!

Before going any further in this chapter, please understand that a goal or a dream in life is not measured by how big it is or by how many people it influences. It is measured by its degree of faithfulness to what God has called you, and only you, to do. This chapter focuses on helping you to name the dream for your life that God has placed upon your heart.

There is one more piece to this. Because our understanding of a pilgrimage is always forward-focused, where we have been does not matter as much as where we are going. Our past does not disqualify us. God can use anyone to accomplish his purpose, and God will forgive anyone who sincerely repents. People who have hated God, let down their families, suffered addiction, made terrible choices, failed in their chosen careers, lied, cheated, stolen, and even persecuted Christians can all be used by God once they have experienced confession and forgiveness. This is hard to understand and believe in a world that likes to hold grudges and "settle scores." Many people find it very hard to believe that God really does offer forgiveness, or that when the slate is wiped clean, it really is a new start. It can be hard to understand what Jesus is talking about in the parable of the laborers in the vineyard in Matthew 20. There, Jesus is talking about the kingdom of God and how it is like the owner of a vineyard who hired day laborers and paid them all the same, regardless of how many hours they had worked that day. From a business or economic sense, this story is crazy, but from a spiritual perspective, it is a wonderful promise, a statement that it doesn't matter whether we come to faith in Christ as young children who are taught by loving, faith-filled parents, or if we come to faith after a long and hard life of failure and suffering. When you surrender your life to Christ, you have all of the assurances in the world that you are heaven-bound.

Dream Your Goals

Life must have a goal. To say there is no God-given goal is to say
that God has not created you on purpose. Far too many people
today cannot hear God speaking his goal for them in their lives.
When they cannot hear God's goal, some people assume that
there isn't one, while others substitute it with one of their own,
like fame, wealth, power, or popularity. A substitute goal can
be wrapped up in a career choice, participating in a nonprofit
organization, a hobby, or even the dream of one day retiring
and traveling. Are these bad goals? Not when they are second-
ary ones. When they become primary ones, however, they will
almost always fail us because they are insufficient.

What Are Your Goals?

A career may be cut short by a layoff or disability; wealth can go
just as quickly as it comes; power comes and goes based on the
moods of others; and popularity changes moment by moment.
When we base the trajectory of our lives on things that are transitory, the chances of failure and disappointment are enormous.
Also, if we focus on substitute goals, they also never fit properly
into our lives. Even when we do succeed in them, the victories
end up being hollow.

On the other hand, when we develop proper goals, we are
building on the solid rock of Jesus Christ instead of on the sink-
ing sand of our own desires. Proper goals are not destroyed
by external events or by other people. Our primary goal must
come from God, and when we stay focused on it, our careers,
community involvement, hobbies, and even retirement plans
fall into their appropriate places, and we can keep a proper and
healthy perspective on them. Not only that, but they can be a

lot more fun because they are in our life for enjoyment rather than meaning. In other words, if you are able to keep the main thing as the main thing, then every other thing falls into place, and everything works!

Your goal should be something related to helping, serving, teaching, or giving to others to help them in their growth toward great Christian living. What is the one thing you would love to do or accomplish that you could see yourself joyfully doing long after reaching retirement age? What captures your imagination, causes you to dream, and excites your interest?

What is the single greatest goal in your life?
(And can you connect it to your life verse?)

Serving God

We are called to be in a relationship with God. But what does that mean for you? Is God like a Facebook friend you check up on once in a while? Is God like your closest friend and someone who is on your mind every day? Do you talk daily with God in prayer and consult God in all decisions you need to make?

Additionally, where is your friendship with God going? What is the point of your relationship? Is there the expectation that tomorrow will be different and better than today? Is the core belief that you are partners who will face the storms of life together, no matter what the future brings? Or is it the kind of relationship in which you pretend you have an agreement that you don't bother God and God doesn't bother you?

When we think of serving God, are we thinking about what God can do for us or are we thinking about what we can do to build God's kingdom? Does our serving show our obedience, or does it merely reflect a desire to be in control of our environment? Does our serving develop something specific in terms of a ministry or a church, or are we working to build something for ourselves that we think we want to have in this life?

As you wrestle through these questions, it may be helpful to remember that some of the beliefs we hold are buried so deep in our psyches that they can be hard to really ferret out. And it is very important to remember that we want to name what we truly believe, not what we would like to believe. Only when we are honest can we name a meaningful goal for our work in serving God. If you think that your goal in serving God is to lead a church of ten thousand people for the glory of God, God may not be the first person you are thinking of! If, on the other hand, your goal is to help equip people who are called to serve in full-time evangelism, then this is another matter.

What is your goal in serving God?

_____

_____

_____

Serving Your Church

Let's be honest. Pure altruism is a rare thing. Who doesn't want to feel useful? Who doesn't like the occasional pat on the back? These are all good, so long as they are not what drives our participation in church ministry. Take time to consider what *really* drives your participation in your church. In your quiet moments, what do think of when you see yourself serving your church? What do you see as your purpose in your church? Are you motivated by having decision-making power? By "being seen," showing others a particular skill or gift you have? Is your goal to be in the "inner circle" of leadership? To get the church to take a particular stand on an issue important for you, or to have the church accomplish a specific vision of yours? If your focus is in any area like one of these, then you are focusing too much on what you want and are neglecting what God is calling you to.

But perhaps you are driven by something very different. Are you only active because you do not know how to say "no" and therefore do whatever you are asked? Do you find yourself overwhelmed by the demands placed on you and confused as to why you are doing things that neither interest nor excite you? If so, then you have fallen into a trap of living based on the expectations of others, and you need to find a clergy person help you work past this!

Are you there to work with new believers? To teach children? To serve the poor? To serve others? When you think about yourself in church, is the vision that comes to mind one that focuses on the needs of others and meeting them? This is a very healthy approach!

What is your goal in serving your church?

Serving Your Community

Some people never give much thought to the community they live in. Some appreciate where they live, but do not consider the needs of the community or the common struggles of the people who live there. When you think of your community, what comes to mind? What captures your attention and imagination? Is it the library, conservation projects, historical preservation, local politics, a local nonprofit, a fraternal service organization, helping the poor, or volunteering for an after-school program?

Some would argue that spending time on such activities is a complete waste of time because the world is a corrosive and destructive place that can do more to damage our faith than we can do to help the world. The rise of monasticism, like that of St. Benedict, occurred because people felt that too much contact with the surrounding culture could only damage one's faith. While such risk indeed exists, how can we be faithful followers of the gospel when we refuse to go out and make disciples? Studies have shown a really odd phenomenon that takes place in people's lives. When someone becomes a devoted Christian, the number of non-Christian friends decreases steadily to the point where within ten years, they typically have very few non-Christian friends. With this being the case, how can we hope to evangelize? For a generation, the argument was that we evangelized by having a great Sunday service, so people would find us on their own. (This is commonly referred to as the "attraction" model of evangelism.) It turns out, this model does not work very well, and we saw a generation of decline in most Christian churches. In my community, for example, less than 10 percent of all people attend church on a regular basis. If we are to re-evangelize our communities, we need to be committed members of those communities, and people need to identify our service to the community as a manifestation of our Christian faith. Then doors can open, and we can engage people in conversations about what being Christian really means and about how Christianity is so different from portrayals in the media.

To evangelize means to be where the non-Christians are. To be where non-Christians are, we need to be engaged in our communities on some level, and that service needs to be done in a manner that shows we are Christians following the calling of faith to love and serve.

What is your goal in serving your community?

What are you most committed to?

Think about what you are most committed to. Each of us has things that interest, drive, fascinate, and infuriate us. I know some people who are so focused on a particular thing that most conversations at some point or another come around to it. I have friends who are such political junkies that they repost twenty or more comments or photos a day on Facebook to spread their beliefs about their political causes. If something in your life drives you, that's great, but it is helpful to see your interests in the wider context of your pilgrimage and how they fit into your faith pilgrimage.

Often, our gifts and abilities are markers of what we are most committed to, and even if we can see those clearly, we do not recognize what they point to until we have discovered our greatest commitment. When I took a spiritual gifts class for the first time, I wrestled for a while with what my passion really was about. Then one day while in prayer, it became obvious. I was a builder.

How did I know? As a kid, I loved to build models, but I hated puzzles. My reason was simple: once I completed a model, I had something permanent. Once I completed a puzzle, I'd have to break it apart and lose all of my work. When I was a teenager, I was active in the Boy Scouts and made it to Eagle Scout. While doing this, I led an effort to clean and refurbish the building we were using; I organized a whole series of merit badge classes for my patrol; and I focused on things that would build up the life of our troop. Years later, when I finished seminary and began to serve churches, I realized that I was attracted to churches that had experienced significant long-term decline and were in serious need of rejuvenation. All three churches I served before going back to school were "turnaround" churches. Additionally, I have tended to do my best volunteer work in organizations that needed to be reorganized and rebuilt. Already well-established groups never really interested me.

I had never connected any of these pieces! Once I realized I was a builder, everything else came together, and I very quickly discovered how the trajectory of my life from childhood showed that I was a builder. Even today, I am involved in building an institute, building a new church, helping with the rebuilding of a struggling service group, and building wooden models of sailing ships in my time off.

Once you know what you are most committed to in life, you should be able to see how it has been at work within you from your childhood, as well. In fact, looking for the connecting links in your life may help you in discovering what you are most committed to. Once you have named your commitments, where and how you serve Christ may be named for you!

What is your goal in serving what you are most committed to?

How will you be remembered?

How do you think you will be remembered? When we think about ourselves, we too often give ourselves a break and rate ourselves on what we intended or hoped to do, rather than on what we did. At the same time, we rate others based on our own criteria and are seldom as willing to give them the same benefit of the doubt as we give ourselves. So it may appear vain to think about how others see us, but it may be an exercise that helps us to get a better and perhaps even more objective view of how we may actually be. Others see us based much more on our actions than our intentions. Thinking about ourselves from others' perspectives could be an eye-opening experience.

There has been a long tradition of people thinking about and talking about what would make good epitaphs on their gravestones. The exercise can be constructive in culling our life down to a single sentence. For example, I know an Anglican bishop who wants to have his gravestone say, "Not according to his merits, but pardoning his offenses," which is a line from the communion prayer in the Anglican prayer book. This particular bishop is a very humble and faith-filled person, and this epitaph fits him perfectly. I also have a friend who wants his to read, "I did it my way." Anyone who has worked with him will tell you, anything he does has to be done his way!

What would be said about you? Would it be that you were always there to help? Would it be that the light of Christ shined through you each and every day? Would it be that you sacrificed everything and everyone to get ahead, but now must leave it all behind? It might be interesting to ask five different friends what they think your epitaph should say and see if there is a common thread among what they suggest.

What one-line epitaph do you hope would best describe you?

The Point of It All

The goal of this chapter has been to help you wrestle with some of the questions that can help you both identify the current trajectory of your life and plan where you would like for that trajectory to go from here. We are not helpless in setting the directions of our lives. But, at the same time, we are not fully in control, either. Goals are very important to have and pursue, but with humility. We should do our best and give our all, but we must trust that whatever we accomplish is done with God's favor, and that sudden changes, unexpected surprises, and even tragedies are part of a picture that is bigger than we can fully comprehend. We must trust that God is still sovereign. Our goal is to be faithful to our calling, not to achieve a specific finish line. This is probably highly counterintuitive, because most of us measure success by results and nothing else. We need to see beyond that. We are called to run the race as best we can, but trust that it ends wherever God has decided for it to end for us.

When the Boston Marathon bombing happened in 2013, race officials ordered all runners to stop wherever they were on the course. I spoke that evening with a Red Cross official who had been stationed at the top of "Heartbreak Hill" and who told me what a surreal experience that was. Heartbreak Hill is the last of four hills that happen in quick succession along the course, and it ends near mile marker twenty-one. It gets its name because this is where many marathoners either give up or have to stop running and walk for a bit. The Red Cross official told me that her team stood in front of the medical tent at the top of the hill and directed all runners to stop and to go into the tent. Many of the runners were so disorientated and confused, they had trouble processing what was going on. They were exhausted, and in such a vulnerable position (carrying no wallets, no identification other than their racing number, no cell phones, no access to a car, and no access to money) that it took many a while to understand both what was happening in Boston and that the race officials would indeed ensure that they would be able to get back to their hotels at some point. None of them were able to finish the race that day, and this too brought its emotional consequences. To help runners adjust to the loss, the race organizers announced that all who were unable to complete the 2013 race would be allowed to enter the 2014 race without having to either re-qualify or pay the registration fees.

In running the race of our lives, we do not have to worry about feeling a lack of closure when we stop. If we are faithful in running as best we can, and if we love God and contribute to building his kingdom as best we can, then our reward is spending eternity in heaven knowing that we did all we were called to do. We do not need to reach a specific goal or milestone in God's eyes.

What Is Your Profession?

In wrestling with the questions of this chapter, it is helpful to think about the meaning of the word "profession." The word *profess* comes from the Latin word used to describe a religious candidate for Holy Orders who would profess, or declare publicly, his faith in vows to be made to God and the church. Such a public profession has a finality and irreversibility to it. In professing his commitment, the candidate would literally lie prostrate on the floor in white clothing and surrender his life to the monastery or convent that he was joining. From that moment forward, his life was not his own. To profess took courage and an unswerving commitment, no matter what the future brought.

It is highly unfortunate that this powerful term evolved into the English word "profession," which is now used to describe any job or occupation. It has also expanded to include more variations. A "professional" is just about anyone who is good at whatever job they may have. And if someone becomes an expert in just about any particular thing, they can focus on teaching it to others and be called a "professor." By becoming such broad terms, "profess" and its derivatives lose the power they once had.

In developing your Rule for Life, you need to see your life as your "profession" in the original sense of the word. You are not just working a job to make some money; you are the care-taker (the real meaning of the word "steward") of an incredibly valuable gift from God! You have been called to use that gift in a meaningful way. The only way to truly live is to profess your faith in Christ, surrender your life, and undertake the lifelong pilgrimage that God has called you to in order to contribute to his kingdom.

8

The Incubator of Wholeness

"nemo dat quod non habet"
(One cannot give what one does not have.)

—Latin maxim adopted by law in many countries
(Schwartz 1335, 1378–83)

Having a religious faith can be a funny thing. For many people, it is just a cultural identity. This is sometimes seen among Jews and Hindus who identify with their religion because it is part of their cultural heritage but engage in no spiritual practices associated with that religion. Other people connect to the religion and its values, but they use their religion to act out on their aggression, hatred, and desires for power. This is seen among those who engage in violent persecution, acts of terrorism, and other atrocities against innocent people in the name of religion. A particularly common problem among modern Christians is to proclaim faith in Christ, but to then live lives that show they have been completely unaffected by that faith.

Part of the reason for this is that many of us live our faith according to our temperament and personality much more than according to the call of God. Our personal interests, our character flaws, our hopes and dreams, and even our deepest fears, all get projected onto God. We view God as we wish God to be rather than how God is, and we see God's call upon our lives as being what we want it to be rather than what God truly calls us to. It becomes a matter of our trying to make God in our image, instead of allowing God to convert us to reflect his image.

Sadly, this distortion leads many to live lives that are clearly hypocritical to the faith, and nonbelievers will look to this disconnect as falsity on the part of the religion. When we lead lives that are bitter, angry, judgmental, and self-centered, we send the message to the world that the Christian faith is weak and unable to lead to human growth and development. God's call is to reject this negativity and to find healing, forgiveness, and transformation. We are to give up the rebellious nature that has plagued humanity from the beginning and find its intended state. Our call is to live in obedience to God and sacrificial service to others.

Playing Head Games

How common is it to know someone who has the "right" view of baptism or eschatology (that is, the doctrine about the end of the world), but is a total jerk to everyone they encounter, or to encounter someone who will argue to the death over an arcane piece of liturgy or theology, but then blithely look the other way as lives are ruined by destructive behaviors? I once met a pastor who was convinced that everything wrong in churches could be fixed with a proper understanding of the works of Martin Luther. A few years later, a lay person on staff at the church was found to be embezzling money, and rather than deal with it publicly, the minister was very content to bury the whole incident. The staff person was quietly dismissed and shortly thereafter was hired by another church. My understanding is that the minister then began a new sermon series on Luther's understanding of forgiveness, thinking that this would make everything better, but he never told anyone why he was doing it. The person who committed the crime never faced consequences for the embezzlement, and the parish never understood what had happened to their funds, but the minister felt he had done a wonderful job because he had the opportunity to once again teach about his favorite subject. Though this example is a bit strong, similar rationalizing of behavior happens frequently among Christians, even ordained ones.

It is easier to argue about ideas and principles than it is to work on changing one's life. It is always easier to talk about what "they" should do than it is to talk about what "I" should do. As Leo Tolstoy said, "Everybody thinks of changing humanity, and nobody thinks of changing himself" (29). It is as if we can somehow justify our own failings by focusing more on those of others. I once had a friend who was a pretty hardcore evangelist post the following on Facebook: "We cannot waste a year, a month, a day, or even a minute. We must serve God every second." Later in the same day, she posted that she had reached level two hundred in Candy Crush Saga. She really believed in her heart that her first post was true, but her later post showed the real truth—she had time for games, even though she argued that everything had to be about evangelism. We want to avoid these mixed messages on our Christian pilgrimages. Our goals in life are to confess our faith in Christ so that we can be dependent upon God, to learn how to surrender our need for control, and to learn how to love others as God loves them. In earlier times, this process was referred to as "the cure of the soul," and in this context, cure did not only mean to heal, it meant the process of formation and growth (see Kolbet). Anything that interfered with or distracted from this process was seen as taking us away from it.

Church was originally a place meant to focus on the cure of the soul. This was accomplished through worship, encouragement, learning, and from belonging to a meaningful faith community. In the early years of Christianity, the faithful met in each other's homes and were involved in each other's lives. They knew they were following a path in life that was different from that of most people, and so they depended on each other for mutual support and encouragement as they made their pilgrimage of faith. Their faith, values, priorities, and behavior were very different from those around them, so they leaned on each other in the hard times and helped each other to grow.

As noted earlier, though, after Christianity became the official religion of the Roman Empire in the late fourth century, things changed dramatically. All of a sudden, by imperial decree, everyone was Christian, and churches quickly grew so big that the people couldn't meet in homes anymore. Christians no longer feared persecution or even being ostracized. In a single century, Christianity went from being an outlaw religion to the only legal religion within the Roman Empire, and the church developed an organizational and administrative structure to deal with these rapid changes. Now with a structure that mirrored that of the government itself, "Christian" attention went away from evangelizing the lost, engaging in discipleship, and serving others, and instead shifted to worship (which was almost mandatory so that people could be "seen" as active Christians) and being obedient to the leaders (to maintain loyalty and order). Over the centuries, governments took over more and more of the functions that had previously been associated with Christian mercy and mission (like hospitals, orphanages, and schools). Being a "Christian" shifted away from being something you were and became more and more something you did.

As the centuries passed, Christians continued to become more and more passive. The church came to be seen as fulfilling a civic function (in performing baptisms, weddings, and funerals) as much as a religious one. In addition, the political and religious authorities became intertwined. Kings and princes sought to mold the church in their image, and bishops and popes sought to influence government policy and balances of power. This system gradually became more and more corrupt.

The sixteenth century saw the explosion of the Protestant Reformation. People like Martin Luther and John Calvin first sought to reform the church, but later sought to replace it with what they saw as the ideal model for church to be. Most of the issues centered on doctrinal matters (understandings of what happens at communion, how to conduct worship, what it takes to get into heaven, and so on) and on corruption (centered on church political and financial abuses). This theological crisis also sparked a political one, and political leaders sided either with the Roman Catholic Church or the reformers based on issues related to their own political expediency. Hence, countries like Italy, France, and parts of what would become Germany remained loyal to the Roman Catholic Church, while other parts of Germany and the Scandinavian countries eventually went Protestant. England followed its own path, which left it somewhere in between the Roman Catholics and Protestants.

The key failure of the Reformation was that it left the matters of living the faith on a daily basis untouched. The passivity of the laity and lack of emphasis on living a changed life continued. As Protestants and Catholics went to war over whether the bread and wine of communion literally become flesh and blood, or whether Jesus infuses the elements in a mystical way, they paid little attention to what happens when our actions do not live up to our beliefs, or what happens when we proclaim faith in Christ but live our lives unaffected by that proclamation. Most people still lived with the belief that we were automatically Christian by virtue of where we were born. Evangelism and discipleship had no context, and mission work was something that people performed out in the few remaining "uncivilized" places in the world—so rather than do it ourselves, we would give money to pay for others to do it on our behalf. In far too many churches, the laity would be heard saying to the clergy, "Please pray for me," because they sincerely believed that the prayers of the clergy person were more efficacious than their own. In addition, it was and is still common in Protestant churches for the laity to have a strong belief in the importance of values like poverty, chastity, and obedience, but they see these as things the clergy need to adhere to, and not the rest of the congregation. It is as if through some sort of vicarious suffering by the pastors, the people are somehow blessed.

Perhaps this is why, at the beginning of the twentieth century, the average Protestant pastor was paid as much as a surgeon, yet by the end of the century, a pastor was paid about as much as a kindergarten teacher. The corrosiveness of this passivity on the part of the laity was ignored, and most people engaged in theological discourse did not even see it as an issue needing to be explored.

Other factors contributed to the accelerating decline of many churches in the twentieth century. After World War II, Western society underwent a fundamental transition. The widespread adoption of the car gave people a mobility they had never known. Growing prosperity gave people time to consider things in life that were beyond mere employment and survival, so an explosion in the growth of fraternal organizations, hobbies, recreational opportunities, and local community engagement took place. On top of this, the development and introduction of television to the home made it easier to stay inside than go out with others for entertainment.

All of these distractions competed with church Bible study classes, social get-togethers, and work projects. For some people, these changes allowed for much more church involvement, but others found interesting enough alternatives that they began to drift away from church. By the early 1970s, Americans had developed a sense that churches were out of touch with the needs of the modern world, and this perception accelerated the church's decline. Over the past few decades, as the split between the Christian faith and the prevailing culture has widened, people who have held to the faith have become more and more marginalized, and Christianity has come under a relentless attack in the media.

So to recap: In the fourth century, we saw a sudden and dramatic shift in a single century, as Christianity went from being an outlaw religion to being the only one legally allowed within the Roman Empire. In the twentieth century, we saw an equally dramatic shift, where in a single generation, the culture shifted from looking at people who didn't attend church with suspicion to one where the culture looks at people who do attend church with suspicion. That is quite a change, and the pace of change is only accelerating in a number of areas.

What does this shift mean? Many people assume that if where we are today is wrong, we need to go back to where we just came from. But part of the problem is that we came from an unhealthy place. So to find the correct model for Christian life, we need to look further back. Many people look to the 1950s and 1960s as a golden age for the North American church, but it was not! Attendance was much higher, but most churches were a mile wide and an inch deep. We do not want to go back to that! We need to go to a time when the church focused on its calling to evangelism, discipleship, sacrificial service, and love, a time when there was a great focus on the cure of the soul. This is where the early church helps us the most. The early church focused on helping people develop a mature Christian faith and taught them how to share that faith with others. They did this in the face of a hostile and distinctly different culture. Does this situation sound familiar? Though Christians are not being fed to the lions today, we do face censure and antagonism. If we were to return to an early church approach to faith, what would it look like? That's what this chapter is about.

Faith Is Lived, Not Just Believed

Mao Tse-Tung once wrote, "If you want to know the taste of a pear, you must change the pear by eating it yourself" (27). To know about a thing is not the same as experiencing it. The same is true for faith. Christianity cannot be fully understood only by reading the pages of Scripture; it must be lived. The Bible talks about our relationship with God, but our faith is the living of that relationship. The difference between just reading about the faith and living it is the difference between *knowing about* God and *knowing* God. It is the difference between knowing that God is all powerful and knowing that he is the good shepherd who leads you to peaceful waters. It is the difference between knowing that God can do anything and knowing that God loves you enough to forgive any sin that you have committed in your life. So you cannot just say that you believe the Bible; you have to live your life as a reflection of how the Bible calls us to live. Since we are called to love God, we need to spend time in daily prayer. Since we are called to love others, we need to reach out in love to people we really do not want to love. Since we are called to serve, we need to have active time set aside regularly where we engage in service to other people. This is all quite simple in principle, but we need to act it out in the real world!

There is often a discrepancy between what we believe and what we do. We have values we aspire to, but they often far exceed our actions. We have hopes and dreams about what we seek to accomplish and how we want to be known, but they often get lost in the tyranny of the immediate—chores, deadlines, work issues, family problems, and so on. We can get so overwhelmed by it all that the last thing we can imagine doing is to stretch ourselves in service to others. Instead, we escape into mindless distractions and entertainment.

However, the record of our lives is written by actions rather than intentions. Our impact upon the lives of others is determined by what we do more than by what we wish we had done.

Others remember us for how we actually treat those around us rather than how we would like to treat them—for who we reach out to and help rather than for what we dream of one day being able to do.

This evaluation is very hard to accept. Our natural tendency is to give ourselves the benefit of the doubt, while at the same time holding others to much higher standards. Often, we also assume that everyone else is giving us the benefit of the doubt, but that grace seldom happens with others unless you are very close.

Whether you believe it or not, your life will be given somewhere and to something. The sum total of the actions of your life will build a story that will state your values, your priorities, your commitments, and the level of faith you live with. C. S. Lewis said it best:

> Every time you make a choice you are turning a central part of you, the part that chooses, into something a little different than it was before. And taking your life as a whole, with all your innumerable choices, all your life long you are slowly turning this central thing into a heavenly creature or a hellish creature: either into a creature that is in harmony with God, and with other creatures, and with itself, or else into one that is in a state of war and hatred and hatred with God, and with its fellow creatures, and with itself. To be the one kind of creature is heaven: that is, it is joy and peace and knowledge and power. To be the other means madness, horror, idiocy, rage, impotence, and eternal loneliness. Each of

us at each moment is progressing to the one state or the other." (*Mere Christianity* 92)

We often do not think about our choices as such a grand progression, because we are too wrapped up in living day-to-day to think about the big questions of life.

I am a firm believer in education, but I am against the use of knowledge as a means to hide from the calling of God in our lives. If we do not apply what we have learned to its intended purpose, then we have gained little by the learning. I have seen the following words attributed to St. Bernard of Clairvaux: "Some seek knowledge for the sake of knowledge. That is curiosity. Some seek knowledge to be known by others. That is vanity. Some seek knowledge to serve. That is love." My goal in this book is for all of us to learn how to love more!

Paul dealt with this problem in 2 Timothy when he offered a warning that there are many people who have "itching ears" and who are always on the hunt for something "new and improved" that will make them feel like they have the inside track on a bit of wisdom (2 Tim. 4:3). The problem with this is that in always looking for something new, they miss out on what is true. The goal of this book is not to give you something new or something to scratch the itch. It is to help you develop a Rule for Life so that you can live a life of devoted faith, committed love for others, and dedicated service to building Christ's kingdom.

Life Is a Pilgrimage, Not a Journey

A great example of an intellectual distraction is back in the story of the Garden of Eden. We argue endlessly over whether or not this story is historical reality, parable, or mythical, as if the answer to that question provides us with the most important answer to the story. It does not, because that is not the point of the story. We use these arguments to distract ourselves from the main point.

The point of the story is that humanity is estranged from God. We rejected the arrangement of God being in charge and calling the shots for our well-being and have spent most of human history trying to be in charge ourselves based on the mistaken notion that we know what is best for our lives. The annals of human history are proof of our failure. Self-proclaimed "progressives" will tout the progress of humanity in the past few hundred years, but every improvement in medicine is accompanied by an improvement in how to kill. Every advance in science is accompanied by a new form of pollution or exploitation. Every advance in technology is accompanied by an equally significant de-humanizing problem. To celebrate the advances of the twentieth century is to ignore the most deadly wars in human history, the greatest disparities in income, and the highest levels of pollution ever seen.

We do, after all, need to be honest here! The real question is not about whether we need to surrender control back to God. History shows not only that we have not gotten life figured out, but that we *cannot* figure it out on our own. The real question of life is, how do we get back to God? The best answer for this is to be a pilgrim who makes the long and arduous trip from the broken and fallen world of humanity back to the bliss of heaven, where we were meant to be in the first place.

The image of pilgrimage has had a long history. John Bunyan's *Pilgrim's Progress* has been continuously in print since 1678 and many consider it to be one of the most important books ever written in the English language. It is the story of a pilgrim aptly named Christian who makes the spiritual journey from the cares and values of this world and to those of God and the Celestial City he is traveling to. He faces each of the struggles and challenges of life along the way. At each part of the pilgrimage, he has the opportunity to stop, to quit, or to be distracted, but through his commitment of faith, he makes it through every obstacle and reaches the goal.

This is the key to a pilgrimage. It is very different from a journey. The word "journey" comes from the French word, *journee*, which refers to a day's trip. A journey is short, typically simple, and fairly routine. In fact, the word "journeyman" referred to someone who worked for a day. You make a journey to Grandma's house or to a mall. A journey can take you to a conference or to a campground. The destination may be fun, like Disney World, or it may be tedious, like a convention for actuaries. A journey does not conjure up images of struggle or strain. A journey is not associated with a life-transforming experience.

A pilgrimage is very different. To be on pilgrimage involves a trip with a very specific goal, one that will require intense effort and perseverance, and one that will change who you are in a fundamental way before it is complete. Sometimes people joke that a trip to a seemingly important place is a pilgrimage. You may hear of baseball fans making a "pilgrimage" to Fenway Park. In my own case, I do not visit the Ben & Jerry's ice cream factory; I take a "pilgrimage" to the factory. In *Pilgrim's Progress*, Christian must pass through despondency, temptation, humiliation, the shadow of death, vanity, hypocrisy, and doubt. He cannot avoid or bypass them. He must overcome every challenge he faces.

Each encounter tests him, and each success strengthens him and ultimately assists him in reaching his destination.

Pilgrimages are not easy! Much of them is spent in places we do not want to be. In Scripture, the greatest pilgrimage lessons are learned from the Exodus, the Babylonian Exile, and periods of foreign occupation. The pilgrimage to heaven began with the expulsion from Eden and grinds on, with each generation needing to learn the lessons anew. We seldom grow when we are comfortable. Like Abraham, we must leave our places of comfort and travel to become strangers in strange lands in order for God to have our full attention and teach us what we need to know. This is a noble idea, but often a painful reality.

When we commit our lives to Christ, our salvation is assured, of that we can be confident! I am not talking here about what we must do to be saved. Salvation is a gift from God that comes when we repent of our rebellion against God, recognize the sacrifice Jesus made on our behalf, and proclaim our faith. That is all that is needed for salvation. But after the blissful moment of salvation comes the beginning of the long pilgrimage of faith during which we will pass through tests, trials, and growth experiences. In our pilgrimages, we learn that even though humans have free will, our first true act of faith must be to surrender that free will to God so that God can control our lives. No longer do we sit and plot our careers, decide what is best for ourselves, or follow our own heart's desire. Instead, we learn to pray about everything, to seek God's will for each major decision in our lives, and to shape our actions according to the call that God places upon us.

We must learn to see the world as God sees it. We must see the face of Jesus in people we don't like. We must learn to reach out to people we feel uncomfortable around. To see the world as God sees it is to be both overwhelmed with the beauty and mystery of what God has created and also to be heartbroken for the ways in which God's children have lashed out at God, at creation, and at each other. To see others as God sees them is to want to reach out in love and to help. After all, Jesus did say, "whatever you did for one of the least of these brothers and sisters of mine, you did for me" (Matt. 25:40).

Finally, when we commit our lives to Christ, we commit to developing a life that reflects the life of Jesus more and more each day. This calls for adherence to the Christian moral code, to evangelizing the lost, and to building up the body of Christ. We do not see the goals of our lives in terms of career, wealth, or fame. We see our lives in terms of being the people that God has created us to be. We see our lives through the lens of mortality on earth and immortality in heaven—which is to say, we live each day knowing that this world is not our home!

Our pilgrimage is meant to take us from the broken hope of Eden to the New Jerusalem as described in Revelation 21. Through our pilgrimage, we leave the pain and suffering of independence from God behind and find the joy and glory of an existence that is lived totally dependent upon God, who washes away the marks of rebellion that damage and scar our souls. We find healing for the experiences in our lives that we do not believe can be healed, and forgiveness for the mistakes in our lives that we believe are unforgivable. We let go of the hurts, hates, and hardships that will eat at us like a cancer if we allow them to. We learn how to truly love and to truly live. Being on pilgrimage reshapes our lives so that we become the kinds of people others will want to spend eternity in heaven with!

Over the years, I have worked with many people who have sacrificed their health, their loved ones, and their own peace of mind trying to do exactly what our society has told them they need to do in order to find happiness. They have acted in ways that were selfish and inconsiderate of the feelings and needs of others. As one friend put it, he grew so busy trying to find happiness that he moved farther and farther away from it. It was only after coming to faith late in life that he found what it meant to be happy, content, and to see this life in its proper perspective.

Each pilgrimage is different, but they all share a common destination. In fact, the concept of there being a destination is an essential one for the metaphor of pilgrimage. We engage in the hard work of learning and growth for a reason. If we are not going to fall into the traps of the prevailing culture, we need a clear understanding of and belief in the destination of our pilgrimage. We need far more than an abstract idea that "someday we will go to heaven." Instead, we need a much stronger conviction that we are only passing through this life, that it is only a shadow of the life to come.

C. S. Lewis talked about this in *The Chronicles of Narnia*. In *The Last Battle*, the last of the books, the children learn that the Narnia they knew was just a shadow of the real Narnia. And though the Narnia they knew was going away, they were not to be sad because it would pave the way for them to visit the real Narnia. Lewis was using this as a metaphor for life on earth. We only live on the Shadow Earth today. We may think that it is important or beautiful, but it is all only a shadow of what the real earth is going to be like. He referred to the current earth as the "Shadowlands" and noted that when we focus too much on it, we risk missing the beauties of the true earth. Therefore, we should have no fear or sadness about either the world coming to an end or our own deaths. Because in both cases, we will merely pass from the shadows into the light. We will leave the Shadow Earth behind and finally experience the real earth.

Why We Do What We Do

A personal Rule for Life provides a structure to undertaking the pilgrimage of the Christian life with intentionality and care. Each of the things explored and discussed in this book represents a step in that direction. Some will prove of more assistance than others, and the ones that provide the most assistance will vary from year to year. Your Rule for Life needs to be something that reflects where you have been, the lessons you have learned, and the goals you see God calling you to. It is also a means for a self-regulated accountability that provides the means for being able to reflect on where you are going and how you are progressing.

Returning to Socrates' words, "The unexamined life is not worth living." If we do not reflect on life, we are unlikely to grow. If we are unlikely to grow, then we will be like Jeff from Chapter One, accepting the status quo and not actually participating in our own lives, and we will leave little trace of our having passed this way. By having a Rule for Life and establishing a trajectory for moving forward, we can take the time to see what is happening and reflect upon why it is happening. God uses all kinds of experiences to teach lessons. Encounters with others may be far more important than we first see. Experiences, good or bad, may have far more meaning than we initially attribute to them. If we do not take the time to reflect upon them, we may miss the meaning of the moment and not learn what God is trying to share.

When we allow the "tyranny of the urgent" to control our lives, we run the grave risk of never moving forward. We can spin our wheels in place and think that our frenetic activity means we are moving forward. Busy does not always mean productive! Movement does not always mean progress! By having a Rule and knowing both how we live and where we seek to go, we can better monitor how we are living and whether or not we are moving the way we think or hope we are.

Still, whatever you do, please do not fall into the trap of thinking that you need to set a specific set of goals and then do everything you can to meet them just for the sake of meeting them! Such an attitude would defeat the whole purpose. When I first learned how to pray the Daily Office, I was more focused on making sure I completed each of the prayers every day than on having quality prayer time. God isn't looking for me to say that I have prayed every prayer without missing one in years. He is looking for me to say that each time I come to him in prayer, it is a time of connection and meaningful devotion. Embarrassingly, it took me some time to get past that! This book offers tips to help you along the way; they are not the goal itself.

You also do not want to use reflection as an opportunity to brood over mistakes or to relive pain and failure. This is not an exercise in intellectual self-flagellation. The goal of reflection is to forgive and to learn, to make the most out of each experience, and to help you to grow and become more and more the person God wants you to be. We are not required to be perfect. We are required to have humble hearts, recognizing where we need to grow, and kind hearts, to let the past stay in the past as we build a better future.

The ultimate test of progress is going to be whether you become a person who forgives others more easily and loves others more deeply than you have in the past. The call of Jesus for his disciples is clear. What you know is not the criteria by which you are measured—how you love is far more important. As we learn how to love more, people will be able to see Christianity as a compelling alternative to the vapid nihilism of secular consumerism that dominates our culture today.

Questions for Reflection

1. If it is true that we judge others by actions, but ourselves by intent, can you name an action or behavior of yours that others see as more problematic than you do? What does it mean to recognize this?

2. Can you name the last time you left the Pilgrimage Trail (had your faith so challenged that you were ready to give up)? If so, what got you back on to it? If you are not on the Pilgrimage Trail right now, how do you get on it?

3. How can we be sure that this earth is only the Shadow Earth and that the real earth is still to come?

4. Draw a timeline of your spiritual journey and list the high moments and the low moments. When done, can you see the trajectory of where God has been leading you?

9

When Bad Things Happen

"We can ignore even pleasure. But pain insists upon being attended to. God whispers to us in our pleasures, speaks in our conscience, but shouts in our pains: it is his megaphone to rouse a deaf world."

—C. S. Lewis, *The Problem of Pain* 81

No study of the development of a Christian life is complete without a contemplation of the nature and purpose of suffering. It is the true refiner's fire and acid test of our faith. Christians should be able to find joy in any circumstance; but all too often, a crisis is a faith-buster rather than a faith-builder. Why is this? When confronted with suffering, it seems far too easy for us to shut out everything and everyone around us, to get tunnel vision, and to lose sight of all that is good in our own lives and in the world. When Job was confronted with the loss of his business and the death of his children, he refused to blame God and famously said, "Naked I came from my mother's womb, and naked I will depart. The LORD gave and the LORD has taken away; may the name of the LORD be praised" (Job 1:21). This level of trust and faith may be hard to fathom. Far too many people have developed the mistaken understanding that if they proclaim faith in Christ, they somehow become exempt from the suffering and trials of life. When suffering does come, they feel betrayed, as if God has somehow not kept up his part of the bargain.

Where does this idea come from? Our Christian faith exempts us from hell. It exempts us from the emptiness of being alone and of having no purpose in life. It exempts us from the sense that there is no purpose in life and from the notion that we are not loved or are not lovable. We are exempted from all of these things, but we are not exempted from suffering. The pain of this life, the heartbreak, the physical ailments, and the randomness of tragedy all hit Christians just as hard as they hit non-Christians. In fact, the early Christians were best known for their suffering physical torture and death at the hands of a government that was trying to destroy their religion. The notion that we are somehow exempt from suffering has never been true and certainly is not true now. The issue for us with suffering is one of meaning, not exemption. It is not that we suffer that matters, it is what we do with that suffering that can teach the world about who Jesus is and what it means to be his follower.

The most common response to suffering is, "Why me?" It is a lashing out at the injustice of our suffering, based on the assumption that it is an undeserved punishment for something we did not do. Another way of saying it is to ask, "What did I do to deserve this?" It assumes that there is a certain quid pro quo to the universe, and that every reaction must have an originating action. While this is basically the concept of karma as understood by Hindus and Buddhists, for Christians, suffering is much more complicated. The big danger of viewing suffering in this way is that it either sends us off looking for a cause for our "punishment" or it reduces us to victims who are helpless and can only cry out against our fate.

Another common response to suffering is to grit our teeth and face it with grim determination. People who take this approach might be heard saying, "I'll get through this even if it kills me!" This response comes from the notion that each experience of suffering is an endurance test, and we have to steel our resolve and force our way through it so that we can reach the other side successfully. In contrast to the "Why me?" approach, which concludes that we are victims who have no control over our situations, the grim determination approach concludes that we are in complete control and succumbing to the suffering is weakness or failure on our part. The experience of suffering is a war, and the war is one that the sufferer is determined to win at all costs.

Still another common approach is stoicism. To be stoic is to ignore the experience and the pain. I have had numerous acquaintances over the years receive a diagnosis of cancer and respond to it by keeping it secret, sharing the journey of treatment with no one, and facing each day with the singular determination to not let the cancer affect anything they have planned to do. For people who take this approach, once the experience of suffering has past, it is never to be mentioned or reflected upon again. At most, some maybe whispered about it as a "recent unpleasantness," but it is to recede into the background of their memories as soon as possible. At its core, this approach is really about being in denial and not wanting the responsibility to deal with it.

All of these approaches fail. We are not helpless, we are not in control, and we cannot will suffering away. To experience suffering is part of the pilgrimage of Christian life. God does not spare us pain; he instead uses it to provide perspective, offer instruction, and soften our hearts. Is it pleasant? No! Is it a fun thing to go through? No! Is it useless? No! This is what makes Christian suffering different from any other experience of suffering. For us, it is not just something to be endured or ignored. Our call is to take the experience and make it a transformational one. We should not and cannot be defined by our heartbreaks, our failures, our mistakes, our addictions, or our baggage. These would leave us without hope. Instead, we need to be defined by devotion, forgiveness, redemption, service, and love. The purpose of receiving these blessings from God is to share them with others. The journey into wholeness does not mean that we leave negative things behind; it means that we transform them and grow from them. The experience of suffering is to be one that leads to growth, discovery, and greater Christian maturity. How can we do these things? That is what the rest of this chapter is about.

Let's begin by looking at the negative things that happen in life in terms of three different groupings. There are things that cause stress, things that lead to suffering, and things that are traumatic.

Stress

Stress is a response to difficult, demanding, or unexpected experiences or events. It produces anxiety, nervousness, anger, discomfort, and even fear. These affect us cognitively, physically, emotionally, and spiritually. In limited amounts, like while trying to meet a difficult deadline on a project, we can deal by knowing that the stress will end and we will have the satisfaction of the completed project. When stress persists over a long period of time, there are cumulative effects that can cause all sorts of physiological, psychological, and spiritual damage.

There are actually two types of stress that we encounter on a regular basis: eustress and distress. Eustress is positive stress that is manifested in increased stamina, focused concentration, and motivation to achieve a goal or to complete a task. This stress often is associated with a euphoric sensation (being "in the zone") and leaves few if any negative effects behind. Distress, on the other hand, is negative and can have short-term effects (fatigue, emotional reactivity, insomnia, headaches, and loss of appetite) as well as long-term effects (hypertension, ulcers, and heart problems).

The physiology of stress begins when the brain determines a sensory input to be threatening. This triggers the fight-or-flight response, which involves the hypothalamus, the adrenal and pituitary glands, and the thyroid. The hypothalamus triggers the autonomic nervous system, which increases bodily functions vital to survival, such as heart rate, blood pressure, body temperature (through perspiration), strengthening of the muscular system, secretion of adrenaline, and the dilation of the bronchial tubes. To make these things happen, the body redirects energy away from intestinal activity, tear duct secretion, and reproductive organs. In prehistoric times, the immediate triggering of the fight-or-flight response in the face of danger was essential for survival, but it was designed to be a rare occurrence. Today, frequent occurrences of such responses lead to psychological and physiological problems, and eventually to breakdowns. The processes and reactions that can help in the immediacy of a crisis can actually have a corrosive effect on the mind, body, and soul when they repeat over a long period of time. Humans just are not designed to be constantly in crisis.

Others play an important role in identifying our elevated stress levels, as we can have a difficult time identifying them in ourselves. Until the advent of electronic monitors, miners would bring canaries into the coal mines when they worked. Canaries were especially sensitive to the presence of methane gas and carbon monoxide, so if the canary became sick or died, the miners knew that there was a problem in the environment. For people living in early twenty-first-century culture today, stress is almost normative and such a common part of daily life that we may miss the impact it is having. Family and close friends can help us by recognizing the warning signs for unhealthy levels of stress. The challenge is that if they are correct, they often will offer warnings at the very moment you are most reactive, since your stress will be evident then. Even though it's difficult, we need to heed their warnings.

As Christians, our balanced and Christ-centered lives should be marked by serenity, joy, and love. Prolonged stress is symptomatic of a life out of balance and a sign that something needs to change. Think of the great Christians you have known, whether they are famous, like Mother Teresa or Rick Warren, or perhaps a neighbor or someone you know at church. Christians of deep faith are ones who are focused on their missions, but are not engulfed by stress. They know how to maintain balance regardless of the situations they find themselves in, and they have a clear understanding of who God is and who they are.

A Rule for Life is meant to contribute to building a life of devotion, balance, and service. Any effort at following a Rule should help you move from stress toward serenity. It cannot give you serenity, but it can help you to realign how you view life and how you live it so that serenity becomes more possible. If your Rule is only adding to your stress, then something is seriously wrong! I've heard a saying that goes, "I never knew how heavy my load was until I put it down." A well-developed Rule for Life helps you with putting down that load!

There are both physical and spiritual resources available to help with reducing stress in life. Exercise, time for rest, a consistent prayer life, breaks in the routine of work, letting go of past hurts, working on letting go of the need to control, and spending more time in fun activities and with loved ones all contribute to helping bring greater balance to daily living. Over the years, I have seen people develop hobbies, join interest groups, schedule more family time, and even change jobs in their effort to find greater balance. For me, there are two activities apart from my work and family that help. One is spending time with others (I joined a community service group) and the other is spending time alone (I have expanded my lifelong interest in building model ships). Together, they contribute to relieving my stress and living a balanced life.

Warning Signs of Stress

Physiological	Emotional	Spiritual
Changes in behavior patterns	Anxiety	Inability to pray/meditate
Sudden appetite changes	Impatience or frustration	Loss of connectedness to God
Difficulty concentrating	Displaced anger or grief	Disengagement from religious community
Short-term memory loss	Depression	Loss of a sense of hope
Difficulty in making decisions	Shame or embarrassment	Questioning what once was accepted as a certainty
Self-medication (alcohol/ drug abuse)	Feeling overwhelmed and trapped	
Significant sleep disturbances	Disengagement from others/ isolation	
Speech pattern changes	Emotional numbness	
Tics or spasms		
Significant changes in sexual activity		
Becoming accident prone		
Pain in various parts of the body		

Suffering

Suffering is more serious than stress, because suffering involves pain. The kind of pain depends on the suffering-inducing experience. In our broken world, there are many causes of intense suffering. It can be caused by a broken or failed relationship, medical problems, the death of a close friend or loved one, a job loss, a sudden life change, a deep hurt by a loved one, an accident—the list goes on and on.

An experience of suffering usually drives all other concerns to the back burner and demands our full attention. It overwhelms the ordinary response or coping mechanisms in an individual and can take weeks, or perhaps even months, to fully recover. Typically, suffering is not something that should be endured alone. Humans are just not designed to be alone. We were created to be in community. Community can be experienced in marriage, in a family with children, in one's church, in a neighborhood, or at work. There are many ways in which we encounter and interact with people. Clearly there are times when we want and need to be away from community, but enduring isolation is not a healthy state. Even monks will tell you that despite long hours of silence, the experience of community in a monastery is very intense.

Some will argue that needing others is a sign of weakness. This is an image our culture presented for a very long time. When we were in pain, we were to become like the Marlboro Man, John Wayne, or Chuck Norris, and bear it alone. To be honest, relying on others is not a sign of weakness; it is a sign of inner strength. It is a sign that we are strong enough to let others into our lives and that we trust others enough to be vulnerable with them. Additionally, keeping pain bottled up inside is also unhealthy. When a water tower has too much pressure, the water will find a way to seep out somewhere. It is foolhardy to think that it won't. Suffering is the same for us. If we are unable to share it and talk it through, the pain will find other means of expression and more often than not, these means are ones that will make matters worse, not better.

My first personal experience of death occurred in high school, when my grandmother died unexpectedly. We were close, and her death came as a total shock. I can remember being inconsolable with my family, so an aunt suggested that I take one of her Valium pills to feel better. I remembered my mother telling me that if I didn't let the pain out then, I would pay for it later, so I did not accept the offer. I let the grief, the sadness, and the emptiness flow until there were no more tears to cry, and I was able to come out of the experience in a healthier place. Had I taken something to mask the pain, it would certainly have found some other way to express itself, and I would have had to deal with the complications it brought.

There is also another side to this. People tend to feel better about themselves when they have an opportunity to help someone. Even if the assistance they offer is something simple, the internal sense of knowing we did something kind is good in itself. When a close friend or loved one takes us into his or her confidence to share an experience of suffering, it is an honor to be asked. Being nervous, uncomfortable, or fearing that you will not have good advice to offer can keep you from helping another person. But if you can get out of your own way, you can experience a holy moment. The other side of this is that if we do not allow others into our lives, we will never give those close to us the opportunity to experience giving this kind of help.

The story of Jesus in the Garden of Gethsemane is an example of this kind of help gone wrong! Even though Jesus had spent endless hours with the twelve disciples, he still had an inner circle of three: Peter, James, and John. Those were the three who joined him at the moment of his transfiguration, and those were the same three he asked to stay up with him while he prayed shortly before his arrest. It showed Jesus' trust, respect, and desire to be with those closest to him in his final moments before his arrest. Though they failed in this mission by falling asleep, we can learn from Jesus' example of seeking support from his friends.

Being able to share with and help others is an important aspect of the Christian experience of suffering. What comes next is the key. Once we have gotten the support of others, then comes the time to find out what the lesson is. God does not spare us from the ordeal of suffering, but he also never wastes those experiences; they become opportunities to teach and shape us. I know from personal experience that God has used each of the significant happenings in my life to help me become what he has intended me to become. My parents sent me to a Jesuit high school for a better education than I could get in my hometown, an experience that enabled me to begin the pilgrimage of Christian faith. It wasn't until years later, after I graduated from college and was working for a high technology company, that I heard God calling me into ministry. The theology I had studied as a teenager played an important role in discerning this call years later. My high school education was not an accident.

Another example: I became close friends for a season with a person in one of the churches I served. He helped me to see that I was manifesting the generational effects of alcoholism. Earlier in my life, I would not have been able to hear what this person was trying to share; God brought him into my life only after I had been properly prepared. Upon his recommendation, I began going to Al-Anon meetings, which had an enormous impact on my growth as an individual, and a short time after that, with God's mission accomplished for us, we lost touch with each other.

A third example from my own life came after I finished the PhD program at Fordham University. I had assumed that I would have an easy journey into academia, but it was 2011, and with the economy in deep recession, most university theology departments were on hiring freezes. I had come from a very blue-collar family; I was the first one in my family to earn a masters degree and am still the only one who earned a doctorate. This was an amazing accomplishment for all of us! Yet shortly after graduation, I found myself working third shift at a department store, stocking shelves all night. Each night, as I struggled with why God was allowing this, I would ask God what lesson he was trying to teach me. A year later, it became clear that my contribution to the kingdom of God was not going to be as a university professor. God had other plans, however, and it was clear to me that I could not fulfill them until I learned to stop taking God's blessings for granted. Only when I could see the hand of God in not only each of the important moments of my life, but in the smaller ones as well, would I be allowed to move forward to what God had in store next. I took a long time to fully recognize this lesson, but once I knew in my heart that I did, it was less than a week before an offer came from a publisher to produce this book. I write it with a deeper trust in God and in God's purpose for my life than I have ever had before!

God is not afraid of our suffering. He is also not afraid to let it linger. This is not mean or capricious; it is only out of our own immaturity that we would think that! We need to be mature enough to stop crying out against it like a three-year-old cries out at the injustice and pain of getting a flu shot. We need to see the suffering of our lives in its proper context and recognize that God will use that time for our growth. We just have to be willing to participate in it. Otherwise, the experience is wasted, we don't learn the lessons, and we don't grow, all of which makes God sad.

There are, of course, exceptions to this rule. Some people are prone to self-destructive behavior. They intentionally engage in activities and relationships that will lead to suffering as a subconscious cry for help without knowing it. Others develop a victim mindset and define themselves by their pain. Others are deeply negative people who can only feel better about themselves when they share their misery with others. I have spent an entire career in churches working with these types of folks. I have worked with a number of people over the years who go from one disaster to another. If one thing is solved, they will subconsciously walk themselves into another emergency or disaster so that they can continue to be the victim. These sorts of people wear out clergy! I remember once reading a study that showed more than 75 percent of people in therapy really do not want to do what is necessary to become more healthy. They would rather meet with their therapist regularly to complain about their lot in life. In all of these instances, professional help is needed. It will probably include medical, therapeutic, and spiritual components, but professional intervention will be required because an entire worldview will need to undergo a shift. If you want to know the truth of where you are, ask those who are close to you. If they are honest, you should be able to get a good picture of where you really are with your life. The effort at engaging in meaningful reflection as you develop a personal Rule for Life can also be of enormous help in trying to figure this out.

Trauma

Trauma is a word used to describe things that go so far beyond the ordinary that they are life-changing in one way or another. A traumatic incident is extreme and results in dramatic and lasting impacts, and it is usually the worst experience of our lives. Traumatic events can include experiences of intense violence like armed robbery, a terrorist attack, rape, the horrors of combat, a severe car accident, a natural disaster, or a life-threatening injury. Recovery from trauma is typically not an automatic occurrence; it requires intentional effort. This not only involves professional intervention, but it requires a reshaping of one's worldview to be able to account for the traumatic event.

Typically, traumatic incidents severely impair the person experiencing them. It is common at disaster scenes to see people moving and reacting in slow motion because they are too overwhelmed to be able to respond quickly to what is happening. Irrational or compulsive behavior is also a common effect. The intensity and duration of the experience are primary contributors to how long the symptoms will persist. However, family, social support, and clinical intervention can play a significant role in shortening the duration.

Because trauma is such an affront to a person's worldview, the victim will often engage in a desperate effort to avoid stimuli that will trigger recurrent memories. For example, someone who experiences a devastating automobile accident may be unable to drive afterward. Sometimes the person will experience amnesia about the event or specific details of it. Additionally, the person may develop emotional numbness, withdrawal, and intense personal feelings of guilt that persist for months or years. The person may even develop symptoms of obsessive-compulsive disorder in a futile attempt to regain control over his or her surroundings.

There are a number of other forms of escapism. Some people will strive to become workaholics in an effort to keep too busy to deal with the crisis; others will turn to self-medication in an attempt to numb the pain; and others will turn to addictive behaviors (whether an unhealthy fixation on physical exercise, the study of a particular technical subject, or some other preoccupation). Though escapism can offer temporary relief, it accomplishes little more than masking the symptoms. Of course, the problem has now become compounded by the addition of unhealthy escape tactics.

In recent years, much attention has been paid to the identification and treatment of post-traumatic stress disorder (PTSD). This intense reaction to a traumatic stressor (which often involves serious injury or violence) threatens the very self-identity of the person. The Stoic philosopher Epictetus, said, "Men are disturbed not by the things which happen, but by the opinions about the things" (3). PTSD is an experience so overwhelming that its victims cannot even process the experience within their framework of viewing life.

PTSD has a very low occurrence in the general population and is usually associated with combat veterans. What is less well-known is that it affects as many as 31 percent of firefighters, and one study showed that 74 percent of the cases lasted for more than 6 months (see Beaton and Breslau). The effects of PTSD on both these populations are significant because they show that even people who are trained to encounter traumatic incidents are deeply affected by them. What then does this say for unprepared victims?

Most approaches associated with helping address PTSD involve talking through the experience and trying to both verbalize the intense feelings as well as contextualizing the experience within one's worldview. Though it may at first seem counterproductive to revisit a painful experience, doing so plays an important role in reframing and healing. Bruno Bettelheim, who both survived and then worked with concentration camp survivors after World War II, said, "What cannot be talked about can also not be put to rest; and if it is not, the wounds continue to fester from generation to generation" (quoted in Vegh 166).

Many twelve-step programs have a similar approach and follow the practice of Alcoholics Anonymous in looking at addiction and other problematic behaviors through the lens of lingering generational effects of unresolved problems. The approach to dealing with them is to talk them through, demystify them, and build a new worldview and pattern of behaviors.

Suffering and Life

Understanding the "why" questions of suffering is paramount. The German philosopher Friedrich Nietzsche argued that people who have a "why" to live for can bear with almost any "how" (Tinker 23). He also said, "What does not kill me, strengthens me" (Nietzsche 6). Being grounded in the philosophical and theological reasons for existence and knowing why you are here on earth enables you to properly contextualize the tragedies, horrors, and violence that are so much a part of life in this world. Viktor Frankl, the Nazi concentration camp survivor, wrote, "If there is meaning in life at all, then there must be a meaning in suffering. Suffering is an ineradicable part of life, even as fate and death. Without suffering and death human life cannot be complete" (76). For Christians, it is essential to have a healthy and meaningful understanding of the role of suffering in life.

In the book of Job, that powerful story about suffering and its purpose, we see Job, a wealthy and prosperous man who loved and served God faithfully. He then loses everything he has. His business is destroyed, his children are killed, and he comes down with a painful physical ailment. Three of his closest friends, Eliphaz the Temanite, Bildad the Shuhite, and Zophar the Naamathite, come to help. They spend a week sitting in silence with him just to be with him as he goes through his mourning and pain. This is a beautiful act of friendship, but they then undermine their empathy by telling Job that his suffering must be a form of punishment from God. They believe Job needs to confess his sins and seek God's forgiveness if he wants to be healed. The only problem is that he *hasn't* committed any sins. The more he argues this point with them, the angrier they become, because they cannot conceive of any other possibility for such suffering: Job must be guilty of some sin. For them, sin and divine punishment go hand in hand. This argument between Job and his friends takes up most of the book! Finally, Job cries out to God to proclaim his innocence, and he demands an answer from God as to why he is suffering. Surprisingly, the answer comes in the form of questions that take four full chapters (Job 38–41). God takes that time to explain all that he has created and done and basically says to Job, "If you are so smart and if you were there when all of these things happened, then *you tell me* why your life is as it is!" The entire response of God is crystallized in one verse: "Will the one who contends with the Almighty correct him? Let him who accuses God answer him!" (40:2).

After hearing this, Job responds in the only way possible for someone who has had a direct encounter with God:

> I know that you can do all things;
>> no purpose of yours can be thwarted.
> You asked, "Who is this that obscures my plans
>> without knowledge?"
>> Surely I spoke of things I did not understand,
>> things too wonderful for me to know.
> You said, "Listen now, and I will speak;

I will question you,
and you shall answer me."
My ears had heard of you
but now my eyes have seen you.
Therefore I despise myself
and repent in dust and ashes. (42:2–6)

What does all of this mean? When Job demands an explanation for his suffering, he assumes that it is unjust because he feels it is unjust, that it is wrong because he believes that it is wrong. The answer God gives is unexpected. Instead of explaining how Job's suffering is a consequence of something else that happened, God challenges Job's assumptions and asks Job if he really is in a position to understand much of anything in God's creation or God's purposes for the universe and for Job's life. This is why Job repents! When he realizes that he was trying to put himself in the position of God by making decisions and expecting things to go the way that he wanted them to, the only thing he could do is repent! God is the creator of the universe, and God is the one in control, not us! Because we are finite creatures, we can never fully understand the infinite God and what he does or what he allows to happen. When we accept that reality, we will have a much better perspective on life, recognizing that our task is to love and trust God and to know that we can never have all the answers we wish to have. This is not a case of a parent telling a whiny child, "Because I'm the parent, that's why!"; it is instead the case of God being the creator and humans being the created.

We may not always have the answer as to why we are suffering, and focusing on pursuing the answer to that question may actually distract us from what is really important in the experience. A meaningful faith life must include both the reality of suffering and the means by which to not only endure it but to turn it into a transformational experience. We must be prepared to suffer the "slings and arrows of outrageous fortune" without it damaging our love of Christ and our commitment to him. It is not a question of "Why me?" as much as it is a question of "What is God trying to teach me in this experience?" We must also, like those who have gone before us and those who suffer persecution now, be prepared to suffer the persecutions of this world for our Christian faith.

Conclusion

The Christian life is one of purpose, meaning, and devotion. A Rule for Life helps us to maintain a proper focus and to ensure that we are intentional about how we make our way through our days on earth. Whether we like it or not, suffering is going to play an important role in our pilgrimage. It is impossible to avoid. A proper Christian response to suffering, therefore, is not to see it as a capricious act of a God who seeks to smite us. Instead, we are to see it as an opportunity to draw closer to God and to learn the lessons that he intends for us to learn. It is not an interruption to our pilgrimage, and it is not meant to derail us. It is a part of the pilgrimage, and though no one likes to walk through the valley of the shadow of death, we know as Christians that we do not make that journey of suffering alone. As it says in Psalm 23, God is with us and guides us to a place of refreshment once we have passed through the valley.

Finally, it helps to remember that even if our pilgrimage through this world is marred by hardship, suffering, loss, and pain, this world is not all there is. It is a mere shadow of what is to come. We may be disappointed in our careers, our health, our choices, and our mistakes, but we do not work just to find satisfaction in this life. Our time here is not meant to be spent in comfort; it is meant to be spent in learning the lessons of God, in devotion to Christ, and in service to others. If we have a true and honest understanding of this, then the trials and tribulations we endure here will not distract us from our ultimate goal. In fact, we can even face death and mock it for its true weakness. In a famous poem by John Donne, an Anglican priest who lived from 1572 to 1631, we see the author raising his fist in defiance of death because in the end, death is powerless over those who have the promise of eternal life! Let us live with the same confidence!

Death, Be Not Proud

Death, be not proud, though some have called thee
Mighty and dreadful, for thou art not so;
For those whom thou think'st thou dost overthrow
Die not, poor Death, nor yet canst thou kill me.
From rest and sleep, which but thy pictures be,
Much pleasure; then from thee much more must flow,
And soonest our best men with thee do go,
Rest of their bones, and soul's delivery.
Thou art slave to fate, chance, kings, and desperate men,
And dost with poison, war, and sickness dwell,
And poppy or charms can make us sleep as well
And better than thy stroke; why swell'st thou then?
One short sleep past, we wake eternally,
And death shall be no more; Death, thou shalt die.
(448)

Questions for Reflection

1. What is your typical response to pain and suffering? Do you drive God and others away, or do you reach out for help and support? How does it impact your prayer life?

2. Can you think of an experience of suffering when God brought a lesson to you? If so, can you describe the experience?

3. Is there a traumatic experience that still haunts you and comes into your thoughts on an almost daily basis? If so, can you name it, and can you find a trusted clergy person or therapist to meet with so that you can work through it?

10

The Joy of Rules

"But in your hearts set apart Christ as Lord.
Always be prepared to give an answer to everyone who asks
you to give the reason for the hope that you have.
But do this with gentleness and respect."

—1 Peter 3:15 NIV 1984

At this point, your personal Rule for Life should either be done, or you should be well on your way to completing it. You should also have a better sense of who you are, what being a Christian pilgrim is all about, and the direction God is leading you. This is quite an accomplishment! Please be sure to use the resources at www.truepilgrim.com to help you as you put the pieces together. The website can also help you print out your personal Rule in a size and format that will help you to maintain focus on it. You should at least have a copy for your wallet and a copy that can be framed and placed on a wall. If you think about it, we all have birth certificates to show that we were born, and we have death certificates to show that we have died. Your personal Rule for Life can serve as the certificate that shows you are really living!

The first significant challenge of your Rule will be to avoid neglecting the goals you have established. Remember, the business model of most health clubs assumes that most members will seldom actually come and work out. Most people who join clubs do so with the best of intentions, but they completely waste their money and derive little, if any, benefit from actually joining. Please do not do that with your Rule for Life! If you have followed the process described in this book faithfully, you will have created a challenging set of standards and behaviors for yourself, and it will be challenging in the beginning to stay focused and committed to the process. However, with time, you will find the spiritual disciplines you have adopted will become part of your daily routine and an essential part of your life. You just need to stay true to the process and give God the space in your life to lead you and guide you to where he wants you to be.

As important as it is to have a Rule for Life, it is also important to remember that this Rule is not set in stone. As you make your pilgrimage through life, your spiritual growth, career changes, and even the effects of major life transitions will all cause you to revisit the different disciplines and priorities you have named. There will be times when revisions are necessary and your focus will change. This is normal and healthy. In fact, if your Rule never changes, it may be a sign of spiritual stagnation. The single biggest constant in your Rule needs to be your commitment to following it and your continued engagement in an honest process of reflection and discernment of spirits.

The road ahead is an amazing one. At times, it will be smooth and scenic, and at others, it will be rough and rugged. The road will take you to the tops of mountains and through the very valley of the shadow of death. The road may look hard, but it is the only path that can lead to true happiness, because it is the only path that helps you become who you have been created to be and to do what you have been created to do. Anything else in this life comes up short and is an inadequate expression of life. So do not rate the road by how hard it is; rate it by what an amazing experience it is to be walking with the living God! Every step will be a holy one, and you will go through every experience with Jesus at your side.

There are some key things to be sure you are clear on before laying this book aside and working with your Rule.

Know Who You Are

One of the issues that this book has tried to address is the mistaken sense among many Christians that a holy or sanctified life is only possible for people who live in monasteries or who are just extraordinary individuals. We put people like Mother Teresa and Billy Graham on such high pedestals that we cannot imagine being holy ourselves. This is a terrible mistake and represents a complete misunderstanding of the Christian life! Everyone is called to a holy life, and everyone is called to experience the amazing adventure that God offers to us. Oswald Chambers addressed this best when he wrote:

> We talk as if it were the most precarious thing to live the
> sanctified life; it is the most secure thing, because it has
> Almighty God in and behind it. The most precarious
> thing is to try and live without God. If we are born again,
> it is the easiest thing to live in right relationship with
> God and the most difficult thing to go wrong, if only
> we will heed God's warnings and keep in the light. (358)

It is essential to understand that God created you in his very image. You are a precious and loved child with whom God deeply desires a close and devoted relationship. However, God will not force the relationship upon you. If the relationship is going to be genuine, then you must give your love freely. If you surrender control of your life to him, trust that his forgiveness is real, and commit to following the path he has for you, then your life will be truly holy and sanctified. It does not matter if you are a missionary, an accountant, a minister, a car salesperson, a monk, a store clerk, or a manager. If you are doing what God has created you to do, then you are living the best life you can possibly live because you will be living out your life's purpose. This may sound deceptively simple, but it isn't. A holy life is within the reach of anyone, but it is a life of commitment and effort. Jesus used the image of being a shepherd for his flock of people. A shepherd was someone who not only made sure that the sheep were well fed and cared for, but he also ensured their protection from the various predators that would hunt them. Shepherds were always on guard, and they would even sleep lightly so as to be able to respond to any disturbance among the flock at night. In John 10:1–21, Jesus describes himself as the good shepherd who not only protects his sheep but knows them by name and is willing to lay down his life for them. It is a compelling image, and in Matthew 18:12, he even says he is willing to leave ninety-nine safe sheep to go and look for one lost sheep.

If you know in the very depths of your heart that you are known by God, that you are loved deeply, and that you really do belong to God, then you are in a place where you can hear God and do the work this book describes. If you are not able to, then you need to seek pastoral support and guidance. If you are unable to see what you mean to God, then you will not be able to hear his voice because it will be too wonderful for you to believe it is real. Like the father of the child Jesus was about to heal, you may need to cry out, "I do believe; help me overcome my unbelief!" (Mark 9:24).

Know Where You Are Going

The Christian pilgrimage is not a voyage of self-discovery, self-actualization, or self-indulgence. If you want to seek "your" path through this life, you are operating under the assumption that you have a full understanding of this life and its choices, and that you are the one who can best determine the path to follow. Everything you read in popular culture and everything you hear in the media will reinforce this narcissistic framework. Each of us hears endlessly that the key to happiness lies in being young, wealthy, and cool. We need to know the right people, wear the right fashions, and own the right toys if we seek to find happiness. This worldview turns us into little more than consumers who must always take more and more to be happy. Few people are willing to name this lie. Hollywood perpetuates it, yet it is a national pastime to watch the self-destruction of movie stars. I live in a city where there are some significantly affluent neighborhoods. It is common for people to have very high levels of education and income. Yet this city is full of people who are deeply unhappy and who are medicated for depression and anxiety to help mask their feelings. The lie consumerism tells about what it takes to be happy is so strong that people will continue to believe it, despite all evidence to the contrary. I once heard a preacher say that giving in to consumerism is like a thirsty person drinking salt water. You may think you are drinking water, but the salt destroys all of the value of the water. The more you drink the salt water, the thirstier you get. One of the lies of consumerism is that if you are unhappy consuming, then you must not be consuming enough. You need more. Of course, you can never consume enough to be truly happy.

The Christian pilgrimage, on the other hand, is an obedient response to the call of God. The path we follow and the reasons we follow it are not always for us to know or understand. Our task is to traverse it faithfully and to know that God will teach the lessons we need to learn, and that he will lead us to the place we need to be. This is true for every Christian. In the beauty of God's creation, each of us lives a unique and distinct life, but we are all called to a common obedience to the gospel. That obedience is not static, like holding a certain political view. It is dynamic and interacts with everything we do and everyone we encounter on a daily basis. Holiness is not only about doing great things for God; it is about doing all things, great and small, for God.

Near the end of his life, Paul shared as much as he could with his protégé, Timothy. In a moment of self-reflection, he wrote, "I have fought the good fight, I have finished the race, I have kept the faith. Now there is in store for me the crown of righteousness, which the Lord, the righteous Judge, will award to me on that day—and not only to me, but also to all who have longed for his appearing" (2 Tim. 4:7–8). We know that we are only here for a short time and that we are here on purpose. We must complete the particular race that God has sent us here to run. After we die, we will be able to spend eternity in heaven, where we will be able to reflect on the decisions and actions we made while on earth. I have no doubt that each one of us will want to know that we gave it our all. Like Paul, we too want to be able to say that we did fight the good fight and that we did indeed finish the race that was set before us. Your Rule for Life will help you identify the race you must run, define the strategy you will use in running it, and provide the means by which you can evaluate your progress.

Know Why You Are Going

It would be a terrible mistake to think that this book is all about action. Engaging in activities that serve others and build Christ's kingdom are very important, but the tasks are not ends in themselves. After some limited experiences in spiritual growth, we soon learn that there can be no real happiness without love. Being alone brings bitterness to and saps the meaning from life. Love for another brings purpose to our wanderings and identity to ourselves. God sees each person as being made in his image, and in loving others, we also express our love for God.

In the famous passage from 1 Corinthians 13, Paul talks about just how important love is. He argues that even if we have spiritual power and have enough faith to move mountains, if we do not have love, then our abilities are useless. Love is the strongest force in the universe. It can bring healing, demonstrate forgiveness, curb anger, overcome envy, and build community. Paul argued that at the end of the day, all we have are faith, hope, and love, and the most important of the three is love (1 Cor. 13:13).

Twelve-step programs call on their members not only to forgive those who have hurt them over the years, but also to hold those people "with unconditional positive regard." They are to wish them well, hope for their happiness, celebrate their prosperity, and express real love. If you cannot make amends with those who have hurt you (as well as those you have hurt), then your recovery process will be greatly hampered. Forgiveness is that powerful! And forgiveness is grounded in love.

When you fall into the trap of consumerism, you put the focus of your life on yourself. Love puts the focus on the other, and love wins every time. If we are made to be in community and are called by God to be loving, then this manifestation of love keeps our focus on others instead of on ourselves. It undoes the effects of the Fall and the human desire to be in control and replaces it with a genuine concern for the well-being and happiness of others. Once the Fall has been undone, we can approach the New Jerusalem and know true peace!

Of course, the kind of love I am describing is not just a warm and good feeling. That kind of love passes pretty quickly in most people. The kind of love I am describing is a commitment. It is a promise to stay true and faithful to the loved one no matter what. This kind of love requires tremendous effort and perseverance, two skills that a well-developed Rule for Life cultivates.

Have a Plan

Few Christians ever set specific goals for their spiritual growth or even understand God's call for their lives. Some make the tragic mistake of concluding that being a Christian is little different from being an atheist—they live the same, but just believe in God. Many conclude that we will be happier by memorizing more verses of Scripture, reading more academic theology, or being able to name more of the spiritual giants who went before us. These disciplines are wonderful, but they cannot be substitutes for fulfilling our life's purposes in the ups and downs of daily living. The practice of spiritual disciplines is not drudgery. Instead, they are the context in which we live our faith and make our way through this life. Our Rule for Life becomes our guide as we undertake our pilgrimage. Our Rule establishes the boundaries of our lives and makes it clear where we draw the lines. Picture the kind of compass used in geometry to draw circles—each circle has an established boundary, clearly showing what is within and what is kept out. Our Rule for Life fills a similar role and enables us to name our limits: how we spend our time, who we focus our attention on, and where we serve. For most of us, we have always known many of our limits, but have simply never articulated them. For all of us, a Rule for Life allows a great deal of specificity about how we will live our lives. This specificity can be shared with our family, our pastors, and our closest friends, who can then help to hold us accountable to what we have established.

This is a very big world, and lots of things compete for our attention. Far too many people live in reaction to the things that happen to them. They do not get out in front of life and get a handle on what is happening. They just go from event to event, or deadline to deadline, or crisis to crisis, doing their best to react to each situation, but doing so with no clear picture of what the trajectory of their life is or of where everything is going.

This reactive approach can make it very difficult to see and learn the lessons that God is trying to teach us. We can also struggle to see how the experiences in our lives are connected to create a specific narrative for our lives.

By being intentional with a Rule for Life, we gain a much stronger ability to see the events and experiences of our lives in their proper contexts, and we are then in a much better position to respond to them. A specific Rule forces us to name and identify things that we may already know in an intuitive, but not fully conscious way. By naming our values and priorities and putting them in writing, we can gain a great deal of specificity and clarity. It also helps us to better align our beliefs and behaviors.

Be Prepared for Pain

As we explored in Chapter Nine, suffering is a part of this life. In contrast to our culture, which sees suffering as one of the worst possible things that can happen, Christians view suffering as a tool that can be used by God for transformational experiences. The key is that we need to be open to those experiences when they come.

How can suffering be transformational? The process starts with the understanding that because humans have always sought to be independent from God, it can be very difficult for God to get our attention. We gain a false sense of security and think that our comfort and prosperity are solely the result of our own brilliance, hard work, and charm. In that context, it can be very hard to hear God! When life goes well, we conclude that it is the natural order of things. When suffering of one form or another hits, we are often taken aback because it is unexpected. For many of us, suffering brings a sense of betrayal because life is not progressing as we think it should or as we feel we deserve. Additionally, we become so desperate to get past the suffering that we lose focus on everything else. The pain can become all-consuming, and everything else gets lost in our mad dash to get past it.

Avoiding suffering means we miss an important opportunity. God does not cause the suffering we encounter in life, but he can use it to get our attention and to bring us to a better place. Suffering can remind us of our need to depend upon God; it can remind us of the need to appreciate the blessings and joys of this life; and it can remind us that ultimately, this world is not our home, no matter how much we may like it at any given moment!

Perhaps most importantly, God can use suffering to get us to look at where we are in our spiritual pilgrimage. Are we at a stagnant place? Have we developed traits that are unloving toward others? Are we drifting away from the path God has called us to? Are we engaged in something self-destructive? Paul, in writing to the Galatians, gives what is perhaps the most powerful account of the transformative effects of suffering. He writes:

> We also glory in our sufferings, because we know that suffering produces perseverance; perseverance, character; and character, hope. And hope does not put us to shame, because God's love has been poured into our hearts through the Holy Spirit, who has been given to us. (Rom. 5:3–5)

So the acid test of whether an experience of suffering has been transformative is whether or not it has added to our sense of hope about what God is doing in our lives and in the world. Adversity can be a true refiner's fire, but just as steel is strengthened by fire and gold is purified by fire, Christians learn perseverance and shape their character through the experiences of suffering that inevitably strike. We do not want to become so focused on getting past the experience that we miss the lessons that God is trying to teach. When experiencing a terrible moment in life, our prayer should not just be to ask God to get us through things as quickly as possible; it should also be to ask God what we should learn while in the midst of pain. We should ask God to help us hear his voice, to help us understand the lesson, and to help us apply it properly. I have hit some pretty big bumps in the road in my own life, and asking these questions has brought intense experiences of growth and transformation!

Our experiences shape us in innumerable ways. I know two men whose wives died in sudden tragic accidents. One man lost his wife in a car accident due to a drunk driver, and his life seems to have ended that day. Everything he does and is involved in is somehow connected to the cause of the eradication of drunk driving. He is involved in developing public service announcements, uses his wife's photo as his Facebook profile picture, spends hours tending her roadside memorial marker, and spends the weeks leading up to the anniversary of her death each year focused on nothing else. Sadly, over the years, his children grew estranged from him because they saw him mourning their mother more than they saw him raising them.

The other man lost his wife in an armed robbery where she and one other person were killed. He went through a serious and protracted time of grief, but after some time, he was able to go on with life. He progressed in his career and raised his children. He never remarried, but he was someone who could find the good in life, he could see the beauty of life, and he accomplished a fair amount in the subsequent years. The pain never fully left him, but it did not control his life either. As a result of the experience, he gained a deeper understanding of the transitory nature of life, and this led him to a much deeper relationship with God.

These two people both had terrible experiences in life. One was traumatized by the pain and never moved beyond the moment the tragedy struck. The other suffered just as deeply, but was able to find a context for the pain and a way to continue his pilgrimage through life as a devoted Christian. These two examples are on the extreme side, but many people will go through similar experiences, if perhaps on a smaller scale. A marriage break up, a job loss, a debilitating accident, a public failure, and any of a hundred other things can happen that can become either the defining moments of our lives or experiences that help strengthen us and shape us to continue our pilgrimages in more meaningful ways.

Truly Live Before You Die

This book is about truly living. When you live for yourself, you cannot truly live. Humans were designed by God to need each other. We need each other for procreation, survival, support, encouragement, and advancement. It is natural for us to come together in families, to form communities, and to join groups where folks are committed to each other. When Jesus wanted a structure for his followers, he gave them the church and a set of guidelines about what to do when someone harms the community (as described in Matthew 18). Most of the New Testament is composed of letters to various churches to help them address their problems and live together in meaningful community. Living in community is very hard, and problems inevitably arise.

If this were not true, then most of the New Testament would not have been written. It is through the hard challenges we face while working with others, learning to love people who drive us crazy, and serving people we want nothing to do with that we become more mature Christians.

Two of the dominant uses of the Internet show both the bad side and good side of human community. On the bad side, one of the biggest categories of the Internet is pornography, which is about using others for personal gratification without true regard for the other. On the good side, we have seen the rise of social media, which allows people who otherwise would have lost touch, or perhaps never even met, to connect with one another. However, an interesting side note to social media is that despite all of the connections it enables us to make, studies are now showing that too much time spent on social media sites can lead to higher rates of depression. This trend shows that though increasing social media connections is a good thing, they cannot be a substitute for face-to-face time spent on our relationships.

In the New International Version of the New Testament, the word disciple, in singular form, appears 28 times. The plural form, disciples, appears 266 times (Dean 176). What does that tell us? It demonstrates that the normal context for discipleship is that growth happens with others. Spiritual growth is a very difficult thing to do alone. For most people living in the Americas or Europe, this is counterintuitive because of the prevailing and mistaken notion that faith is just between God and each individual. Being Christian is not just about "me and Jesus," it is also about being in community and building Christ's kingdom together. It is about bringing more and more people into the family of God and sharing the struggles and joys of life together.

A Fond Farewell

It is my deepest hope and earnest prayer that this book has been helpful to you as you wrestle with God's call and plan for your life. Even if you have followed each step described here as scrupulously as you could, I'm sure there are lingering uncertainties that will take long sessions of prayer and deep conversations with others to discern. This has certainly been the case in my own work with developing a Rule! Fortunately, uncertainty is part of the process and gives God room to continue working on us, helping us learn about the path of our pilgrimage. Please be sure to use the resources at www.truepilgrim.com to help you in this process.

As the Jesuits say in their motto, everything we do is done, "Ad majorem Dei gloriam inque hominum salutem," which when translated from the Latin means, "For the greater glory of God and the salvation of humanity." As we grow in our love for God and commitment to others, people who are lost and struggling with the lies of the prevailing culture will see more and more that we live life by a different set of rules. The resulting happiness is something that they will most certainly want to share, and you will find that opportunities for evangelism arise in the most unexpected places. So be prepared to give an answer when asked.

Thank you for letting me share this time with you. I hope to be invited into your life through another book in the near future!

Questions for Reflection

1. What originally induced you to read this book? How has it met or not met your goals?

2. Have you created your Rule for Life yet? If so, who will you ask to hold you accountable to it? If not, what is causing the delay?

3. Write out your Rule for Life here.

Bibliography

Beaton, R., S. Murphy, and W. Corneil. "Prevalence of Posttraumatic Stress Disorder Symptomatology in Professional Urban Fire Fighters in Two Countries." International Congress of Occupational Health, Stockholm, 1996.

Breslau, N., R. Kessler, H. Chilcoat, L. Schultz, G. Davis, and P. Andreski. "Trauma and Posttraumatic Stress Disorder in the Community." *Archives of General Psychiatry* 55 (1998): 626–633.

Brother Lawrence. *The Practice of the Presence of God*. New Kensington, PA: Whitaker House, 1982.

Bugbee, Bruce. *What You Do Best in the Body of Christ: Discover Your Spiritual Gifts, Personal Style, and God-Given Passion*. Grand Rapids, MI: Zondervan, 2005.

Bunyan, John. *Pilgrim's Progress*. Reissue Edition. Oxford: Oxford University Press, 2009.

Chambers, Oswald. *My Utmost for His Highest*. Expanded Edition. Grand Rapids, MI: Discovery House Publishers, 1994.

Colson, Charles, and Nancy Pearcey. *How Now Shall We Live?* Carol Stream, IL: Tyndale House Publishers, Inc., 1999.

Dean, Kendra, Chap Clark, and Dave Rahn. *Starting Right: Thinking Theologically About Youth Ministry*. Grand Rapids: Zondervan, 2010.

Donne, John. *The Works of John Donne*. Vol. VI. Edited by Henry Alford. London: John W. Parker, 1838.

Epictetus. *Enchiridion*. Edited by George Long. Mineola, NY: Dover Publications, 2004.

Foster, Richard J. *Celebration of Discipline: The Path To Spiritual Growth*. San Francisco: HarperSanFrancisco, 1988.

Frankl, Viktor. *Man's Search for Meaning: An Introduction to Logotherapy*. 3rd ed. New York: Touchstone, 1984.

Gallagher, Timothy M. *The Discernment of Spirits: An Ignatian Guide for Everyday Living*. New York: Crossroad Publishing, 2005.

Golding, William. *The Lord of the Flies*. London: Faber and Faber, 1954.

Harrison, George. "Any Road." *Brainwashed*. Burbank, CA: Dark Horse/EMI, 2002.

Keller, Helen. *The Open Door*. New York: Doubleday, 1957.

Kolbet, Paul R. *Augustine and the Cure of Souls: Revising a Classical Ideal*. Notre Dame, IN: University of Notre Dame Press, 2009.

Lewis, C. S. *The Chronicles of Narnia: The Last Battle*. New York: Scholastic Press, 1994.

——————. *Mere Christianity*. New York: Macmillan, 1952.

——————. *The Problem of Pain*. New York: Macmillan, 1962.

Mother Teresa of Calcutta. "And You, Who Do You Say That I Am?" *Jubilee Magazine* 4 (September 1997): 10.

Nietzsche, Friedrich. *The Twilight of the Idols and The Antichrist*. Translated by Thomas Common. Digireads.com, 2009.

Pennington, M. Basil. *Centered Living: The Way of Centering Prayer*. Liguori, MO: Liguori/Triumph, 1999.

Plato. *The Apology of Socrates*. London: F. E. Robinson & Company, 1901.

Schwartz, Alan, and Robert E. Scott. "Rethinking the Laws of Good Faith Purchase." *Columbia Law Review* 6.111 (2011).

Smietana, Bob. "Running Out of Miracles: Big Idea Creator Phil Vischer Had His Dream Crumble, But He's No longer S-Scared." *Christianity Today* 48 (May 2004): 44.

St. Augustine of Hippo. *Confessions*. Peabody, MA: Hendrickson Publishers, 2011.

St. Benedict of Nursia. *The Rule of Saint Benedict*. Translated by Leonard J. Doyle. Collegeville, MN: Liturgical Press, 2001.

St. Ignatius of Loyola. *The Spiritual Exercises and Selected Works.* Edited by S. J. George and E. Ganss. Mahwah, NJ: Paulist Press, 1991.

—————. *The Spiritual Exercises of St. Ignatius of Loyola.* Translated by Thomas Corbishley, S.J. Mineola, NY: Dover Publications, 2011.

Thoreau, Henry David. *Walden.* New York: Thomas Y. Crowell & Co., 1910.

Tinker, Melvin. *Why Do Bad Things Happen to Good People? A Biblical Look at the Problem of Suffering.* Fearn, UK: Christian Focus, 1997.

Tolstoy, Leo. "Three Methods of Reform." In *Pamphlets: Translated from the Russian.* Translated by Aylmer Maude. Christchurch, New Zealand: Free Age Press, 1900.

Tse-Tung, Mao. *Collected Writings of Chairman Mao: Volume 3—On Policy, Practice and Contradition.* Edited by Shawn Conners. El Paso, TX: El Paso Norte Press, 2008.

Vegh, Claudine. *I Didn't Say Goodbye.* Translated by Ros Schwartz. New York: E.P. Dutton, 1984.

Warren, Rick. *The Purpose-Driven Life.* Grand Rapids: Zondervan, 2002.

Weil, Simone. *First and Last Notebooks.* Edited by R. Rees. Oxford: Oxford University Press, 1970.